Puzzles, Boxes and Toys:
Creative Scroll Saw Patterns

Puzzles, Boxes and Toys:
Creative Scroll Saw Patterns
Percy W. Blandford

TAB BOOKS
Blue Ridge Summit, PA

FIRST EDITION
FIRST PRINTING

© 1991 by **TAB Books**.
TAB Books is a division of McGraw-Hill, Inc.

Library of Congress Cataloging-in-Publication Data

Blandford, Percy W.
   Puzzles, boxes, and toys : 39 creative scroll saw patterns / Percy
W. Blandford.
    p.   cm.
   ISBN 0-8306-6706-7 (h)   ISBN 0-8306-8706-8 (p)
   1. Wooden toy making. 2. Jig saws. 3. Puzzles. 4. Boxes,
Wooden. I. Title.
TT174.5.W6B57 1991
684'.083—dc20   91-10782
                                   CIP

TAB Books offers software for sale. For information and a catalog, please contact
TAB Software Department, Blue Ridge Summit, PA 17294-0850.

Acquisitions Editor: Kimberly Tabor
Technical Editor: Steve Moro
Production: Katherine G. Brown
Book Design: Jaclyn J. Boone
Cover Design: Lori E. Schlosser

Contents

Introduction

Scroll saws, as we know them today, are a comparatively recent development, and their potential is not always realized. Fine saw blades that could be tensioned in a frame and made to follow intricate shapes have been available for a long time. At first they were used in hand frames, and what was possible with such simple tools in skilled hands can be seen in the decoration of some antique furniture. Then came the treadle-operated fretwork machine, however; it is too easy to regard a scroll saw as just an updated version of that.

There is some confusion over the name. The tool has been called a *jigsaw* and some makers still use that term. A jigsaw puzzle will probably always be called that, even if it is cut on a scroll saw. The word *jigsaw* may now be applied to the portable power tool with a blade held only at one end and used for fairly coarse curved cuts. It may also be called a *saber saw*. A bandsaw will make some of the same cuts as a scroll saw, but it is not as versatile because it cannot make such fine cuts, nor cut internally.

Possibly because of the fretwork machine image, many workers regard a scroll saw as just a means of cutting intricate shapes in thin wood. Many designs and patterns offered for scroll saw work are limited to those things. Too often, masses of published intricate patterns are found without practical applications.

Of course, a scroll saw will do all of the aforementioned—and much more. It will cut wood more than 1-inch thick; some machines will cut much more. It will cut at an angle and maintain that precise angle while following a complicated outline. It will cut veneers precisely. It will cut metals and plastics from the thinnest to thickest sections.

While remembering that it will cut other materials, wood will concern most users of a scroll saw; in fact, its potential for cutting thicker wood has not been fully exploited. In this book there are projects that include the fretwork type of operation, but there are others in which shaping is done in wood of more substantial sections.

Most owners of a scroll saw will be using it as part of their shop equipment, so it is assumed there are facilities for drilling, planing and other operations required to complete a piece of work that might also involve a considerable use of the scroll saw. An application of the scroll saw that is not always appreciated is its ability to cut many joints that would otherwise involve other tools. As you get to know your scroll saw, you will find increasing uses for it.

Many of the 39 projects in this book also include several possible variations in pattern and design, so it is hoped you will find some other ideas for things to make using your scroll saw. The chapters form convenient groupings, but some projects, or a variation of them, might also be applicable in other groupings. In any case, you will probably start developing your own ideas, based on things you see in this book. There is great satisfaction to be had out of making something which follows a published design, but there is an even greater satisfaction to be derived from producing something which is unique to you.

A pattern cut out on its own may look good, but it might be of little use. Make it into something and you have an article which should be useful and attractive. The scroll saw allows you to give shape to something that might otherwise look too severe. This is a book of things to make and not just shapes to cut. I hope I have shown you how to use your scroll saw to its fullest potential.

One

Preparations

This is a book of projects and design—not an instruction manual on how to use your scroll saw. It is assumed you have sufficient knowledge to set up your scroll saw and work with it to achieve satisfactory results. However, there are a few points on project constructions and their variations which are covered in this chapter.

Some instructions applicable to particular projects are given where most appropriate. In general, step-by-step instructions are self-contained. All sizes quoted on drawings, instructions, and materials lists are in *inches*. Dimensions quoted for wood are finished width and thickness, but an extra measure is given on most lengths to allow for trimming to remove possible splits and shakes. If you use plywood, a hardwood gives better results than softwood. Some imported hardwood plywood is in metric thicknesses. Close approximations are as follows: 6mm = $\frac{1}{4}$ inch, 8mm = $\frac{5}{16}$ inch, 9mm = $\frac{3}{8}$ inch and 12mm = $\frac{1}{2}$ inch.

ENLARGING

Ideally, prepared patterns would be fullsize, so you can stick the paper to the wood and cut the shape. Because of page size restrictions that is impossible in this book. The problem also occurs if you adapt an illustration from a magazine or elsewhere. It is unlikely to be the size you want.

Some office copying machines will enlarge or reduce a drawing. That may be your answer to preparing a pattern to cut, if what you want is within the scope of the machine.

An alternative is to use squares. If you cover the drawing with a grid of squares and draw another grid of squares proportionately bigger, you can note where lines on the original design cross lines on its squares. Then, mark estimated positions on the other squares, and join them freehand to get an enlarged reproduction.

With most patterns in this book, a grid of squares covering the drawing is already provided. If you prepare a grid of squares of the size indicted on plain paper, you are ready to draw a reproduction of the pattern to the size intended. If you want your drawing to be a different size, this is the stage where you arrange it. If the pattern is designed to be enlarged on 1-inch squares, but you want to make it bigger, draw your grid with 1¼ inches, 1½ inches, or whatever proportion you want the increase to be.

If you want to alter the pattern to a different proportion between length and breadth, possibly to fit a particular space, draw rectangles instead of squares, such as 1 inch × 1¼ inches. Do not try to distort a pattern too much, but moderate variations are possible.

As an example of enlarging, suppose the grid on the book drawing is marked as 1-inch squares, but as printed they are smaller (FIG. 1-1A). Draw a grid of the same number of squares with 1-inch sides (FIG. 1-1B). Note where pattern lines cross grid lines (FIG. 1-1C). Estimate proportional distances along the appropriate squares of your grid, and mark the points (FIG. 1-1D). Do this with every crossing of the pattern and its reproduction. Join the points on the larger grid. Do this freehand in most parts, but for long flowing curves you might find it better to bend a thin lath through the points, while a helper draws a line along it.

If the design is symmetrical and you print or draw the reproduction on tracing paper, that can be turned over to show through the pattern the other way. If the design is repeated, as with a shaped border, it is wisest to make a template from card or hardboard (FIG. 1-1E), and move it along for marking as often as necessary to ensure uniformity.

SAW BLADES

The number of different types of blades available can be bewildering. Suppliers provide tables showing their range of blades and recommended applications. For best results on the variety of projects in this book, you need blades of many types offered.

There are some general considerations. A narrow blade will turn in a very small radius. A wider blade may not turn as tightly, but it will be much stronger. If you want to follow a straight line or a long sweeping curve, it will be much easier to keep to the line with a broad blade.

For best results, you should try to have at least three teeth within the thickness of the wood, which means the teeth should be at a fine pitch for very thin wood. There can be as many as 60 teeth per inch in some blades, so you should be able to get at least three teeth in the thinnest wood.

The usual saw blade has plain ends, to be held by the grip of a clamping arrangement. There are also blades with a small pin across each end. These are blades with coarse teeth and a width near ⅛ inch that were originally intended for

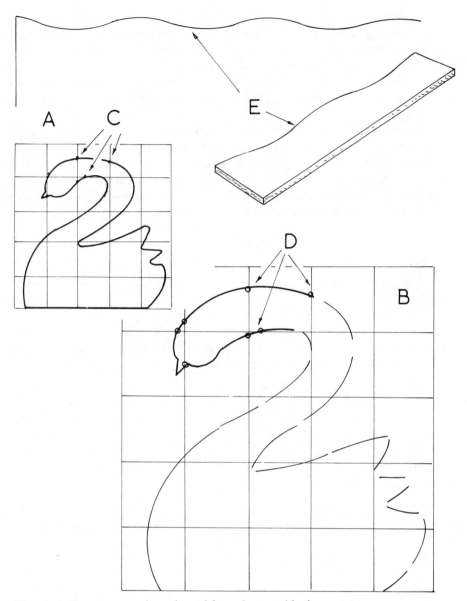

Fig. 1-1. Patterns may be enlarged by using a grid of squares.

use in a hand coping saw frame. If your machine will take these blades, they are useful for heavy cuts in thicker wood.

Blades for cutting metal have very fine teeth. Do not use one of these blades on wood or plastic, as the teeth will clog. The best metal-cutting blades are used in hand frames by jewelers, but they can also be used in a scroll saw.

It might be possible to cut plastics with a blade intended for wood, but the types of plastics vary. Consult the blade makers' recommendations. You will find they also recommend blades for many materials you do not normally expect to cut, such as paper, bone, ivory, brake lining and felt.

You can get skip-tooth blades. On one of these blades alternate teeth are eliminated; this is claimed to provide better sawdust clearance with faster and cooler cutting.

Obtain blades that appear to cover all your needs; then, experiment with them on scrap pieces of wood of the types you intend using in various thicknesses. Note the effects, and keep a record of your personal choice for particular circumstances. You will then have your own guidelines and can reduce the range of blades you need. Note the life expectancy of a blade type. It is of little use favoring a blade for its satisfactory cut if it does not last long.

CUTTING

When making a vertical cut, turn the blade on the spot at a corner. The angle will lose in sharpness by the width of the blade. This radius may be so minute that it does not matter.

If it is an external cut, get a sharper point by running off into the waste wood, and coming back to start the other way (FIG. 1-2A). If it is an internal corner or point, cut up to the corner along one line; then, back off and cut across the waste part to approach the corner along the other line (FIG. 1-2B).

Fig. 1-2. Corners are cut sharper if approached from two directions.

For sloping cuts, trying to turn on the spot at a corner is risky, and you could break the blade as it turns on the spot at the top but follows a small curve underneath.

Plan your cutting program so you always have something to hold. It is usually best to do piercing before cutting a profile. Watch for narrow cross-grain parts that might be damaged. Leave cutting at least one side of such a part until most other work has been cut.

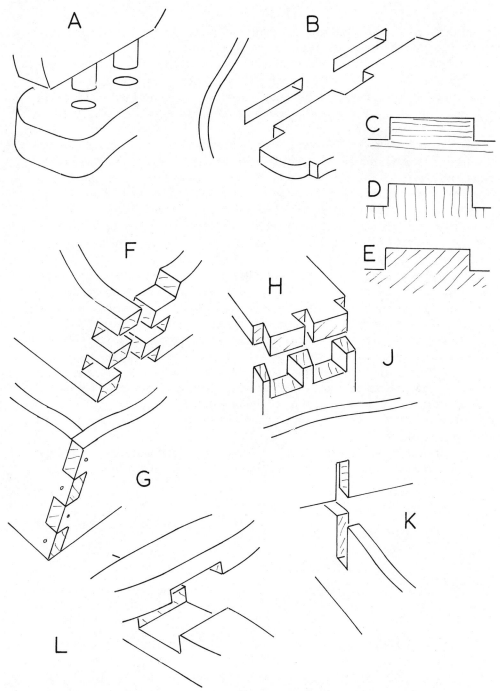

Fig. 1-3. Many joints can be used in scroll saw constructions.

JOINTS

If the work on the scroll saw is only part of some piece of furniture or other article, you may choose to select and cut joints by some other means, but there are a number of joints which can be made entirely or partially with a scroll saw.

For general assembly, without using the scroll saw, doweling is simple and convenient, as you only need a prepared dowel rod and a drill with a bit of the right size. Choose dowel diameters about half the thickness of the wood and have at least two in each joint (FIG. 1-3A).

For joints between scroll-sawn parts it is usually possible to include mortises and tenons, which can be cut completely with the scroll saw. The mortises may be fairly long, but do not cut away too much wood. Instead of a long mortise it is better to use two widely spaced shorter ones (FIG. 1-3B). Try to avoid arranging a tenon with the grain across (FIG. 1-3C), which would be weak. It is better for the grain to be the other way, (FIG. 1-3D); where two tenons have to be square to each other you can get sufficient strength in both by having the grain diagonally (FIG. 1-3E).

A comb joint (FIG. 1-3F) is strong because of its considerable side grain glue area. You can cut the parts completely by careful use of a scroll saw. An alternative, which is less troublesome, is a finger joint (FIG. 1-3G). Cut it in the same way, but secure it with glue and a pin centrally in each finger.

Dovetail joints can be cut almost completely with a scroll saw. The tails (FIG. 1-3H) are straightforward cuts. The slope of the pins can be cut with the table tilted (FIG. 1-3J). With a table that will tilt back to front or can mount the blade to cut crosswise when the table is tilted the other way, you can cut across the bottoms of the sockets right into the sloping sides of the pins. Otherwise, you will have to cut squarely across with the narrow sides of the sockets upwards; then, finish with a little hand work.

Halving joints on edge (FIG. 1-3K) are simple cuts. Halving joints in the flat direction (FIG. 1-3L) can be scroll sawn if the thickness is not too great.

Two

Simple Cutouts

Anyone using a scroll saw, for the first time will find it worthwhile merely cutting wood in various thicknesses and types, within the whole range of available blades. This applies even if you have had plenty of experience with other hand and power tools, because cutting with a scroll saw is a different technique. The way to master it and realize its potential is to cut wood in various ways.

As most of the applications of a scroll saw are in cutting shapes in flat pieces of wood, that is where practice is valuable. While practicing, you will soon discover that you can get a lot of satisfaction out of producing cutouts in many forms.

Once you have learned to control the saw, make it cut exactly as you want it to, and pierce holes that finish with the shape shown in the original pattern or design, you can start to make articles which are complete in themselves.

Start with the thinner woods. Plywood is good practice material. Its edges, cut with a fine saw, might be considered to have a beauty of their own. Progress to thicker wood and let the blade cut at its own speed. It may not be very fast, but the results are worth the time taken.

Jigsaw puzzles are good practice pieces. You do not have to cut with great precision; the results are welcome and acceptable by people of all ages. When you move on to thicker wood and make cut out animals and other forms as solid jigsaw puzzles, you will have produced something rather unusual; moreover, you will begin to realize the potential of the modern scroll saw compared with the earlier, more limited fretwork machine.

Not all the work done on a scroll saw need be small, but at first you can get plenty of satisfaction and experience out of making things from pieces of wood that might be considered too small to be of any use for other branches of woodworking. With a scroll saw you can make an attractive piece of jewelry or decoration out of a couple of square inches of thin wood.

Although most simple cutouts are best made in wood, as it is an easy medium to cut, try making some cutouts from metal and plastic. With the right blades and some patience you can produce shapes that would be difficult to obtain in any other way.

If you are new to scroll sawing, spend some time mastering work of the type described in this chapter. This will be satisfying in itself, but it will also prepare you for some of the more ambitious projects described later.

JIGSAW PUZZLES

Among the most popular uses of the predecessors of the scroll saw, the hand or treadle fretsaw, was the making of jigsaw puzzles. These are still worthwhile projects. They may vary from simple puzzles with bold pictures and large parts for use by a child, to elaborate and detailed pictures with hundreds of parts. There can be educational puzzles and others which provide clues to competitions. Three-dimensional and structural puzzles are possible, and discussed later, but only flat pictorial puzzles are mentioned here.

A puzzle consisting of a picture glued on wood is more durable than the pressed card puzzles currently available. In short, if the puzzle is to be used by many people, including children, your wood puzzle will be much more suitable.

The best material is thin hardwood plywood for most puzzles, not more than ¼-inch thick, although, a child's puzzle of a few large parts may be thicker. You could use hardboard. Thin solid wood is not so suitable, because of the risk of warping.

Make a jigsaw puzzle from almost any picture. If the paper is thin, it might distort from the moisture in the glue. At the other extreme, it might be difficult to make pictures on card adhere all over, so edges may curl after cutting. A picture on paper of moderate substance is best. Have as much glaze as you like on the picture side, but excessive gloss on the back may interfere with good adhesion.

There are glues described as suitable for paper and wood. One of these or a rubber cement may do, but a fairly liquid wood glue will be stronger. On most woods you can glue without advance preparation, but with some very absorbent woods and hardboard, so much glue may soak in with a single application that the paper may not hold very well. In that case, apply a coat of glue to the wood and let it dry; then, lightly sand it and apply another coat to hold the paper.

The base plywood could be cut to the same size as the paper picture, but it is easier to have it slightly oversized at first; then, plane the edges after the paper has been glued on. This allows you to take care of slight discrepancies; furthermore, you get true matching edges of plywood and paper. Use a finely set hand plane held diagonally to the edge, so you take a slicing cut from the paper towards the wood.

To avoid air bubbles being trapped under the paper, lower it on from one edge and stroke it down gently (FIG. 2-1A). Finally, rub with a circular action from the center to the edges, using a piece of clean scrap paper over the picture. Allow the glue to harden before planing, and possibly sanding, the edges.

There is no need to mark out the cuts. You can go across freehand. In that way you get variations in the cuts and no two pieces are likely to complicate assembly by being alike. Many parts may be almost alike; this is one of the factors that makes solving the puzzle interesting.

If you have never cut a jigsaw puzzle, experiment first on some scrap plywood. If you cut wavy lines across both ways (FIG. 2-1B) there is nothing to keep the pieces in position, unless the puzzle will be enclosed in a border. It is more usual for a puzzle without a border to have pieces interlocking. To do this you have to include a somewhat rounded dovetail joint on each side of each piece (FIG. 2-1C). You soon get into the habit of doing this as you work your way across. The important consideration is to decide on the approximate size of each piece, because

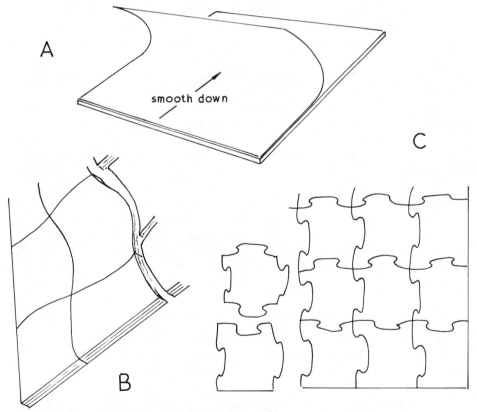

Fig. 2-1. Jigsaw puzzles are better cut interlocking.

you have to include the interlocking action in each edge. Pieces could vary in size, but it is usual to avoid too great a difference. For a child's puzzle, the pieces could be 3 inches or more across, but for most puzzles you will probably settle for less than half this measurement. To give you an idea of numbers, divide the overall size by the intended size of a piece. Consider a picture 12-inches square and pieces about 1½ inches each way. That gives eight in each direction and a total of 64, so with 1-inch pieces you would get 144. Pencil the edges as a guide to evenly spaced starting cuts.

The thickness and coarseness of the saw blade depends on the type of plywood and the intended use of the puzzle. For a child's puzzle, you need wider gaps and an easier fit between pieces; for adult use, you can make the puzzle with closer joints. It will probably be advisable to experiment with saw types on scrap plywood of the sort to be used in the puzzle.

When you have made all the cuts one way, it is helpful to assemble the strips on a piece of card; then make the cuts the other way.

A puzzle for a child need only have a few large parts. For the youngest child these need not interlock, but a frame shows the child the finished size, as well as keeping the parts together. Eight to twelve parts (FIG. 2-2A) are all that the young-ster can assemble without becoming frustrated. Cut the border out of a piece of plywood, or use strips of solid wood on a base (FIG. 2-2B). Do not make the border too tight a fit on the completed puzzle.

You could use a map as an educational jigsaw puzzle. A state map might be made into an interlocking puzzle, with the roads and other features as guides to how the pieces make up the picture. You might cut a state into counties to teach the positions of boundaries. These parts would not interlock, so there would have to be a frame.

You could do the same with the whole country, with each state cut to shape. To make it more difficult, cut the state shapes without any pictures on the surface to guide the user. Pieces could be stained or painted differently, so the result is a patchwork of colors in the form of states. You may choose to emphasize only part of the country. If there is sea, that would be blue and could have interlocking parts, but the whole assembly would need a frame (FIG. 2-2C). How much detail you put into state outlines depends on the size of the puzzle. Avoid sharp and narrow outlines, such as river estuaries; they will have to be eased to moderate curves, which will be stronger.

ANIMAL SHAPES

Animal or bird shapes may be cut from wood of various thicknesses, in sizes from an inch or so across as ornaments, to quite large toys. With a suitable blade you can cut the edges cleanly, so little further treatment is needed. The range of patterns is almost endless. If you draw the shapes yourself, use prepared patterns or find illustrations in books and magazines.

It is possible to cut a realistic outline of some animals, but other shapes may have to be modified a little. It would be unwise to try to put a lot of feather detail

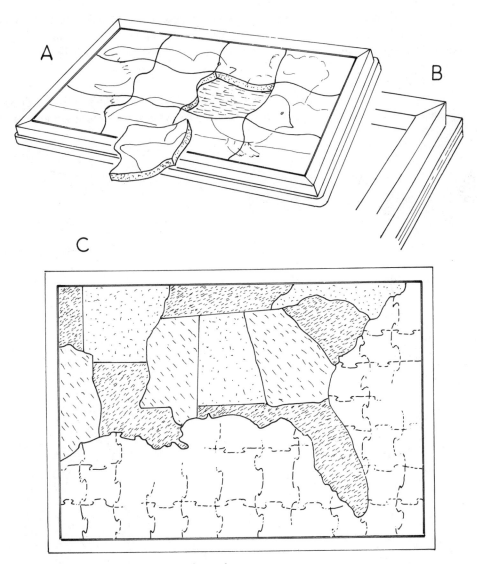

Fig. 2-2. Jigsaw puzzles may be framed.

on a bird or a slender trial on an animal. Some animals or birds, particularly if intended as toys, might be more like cartoon representations.

Many animal cutouts are effective without any surface decoration, although a dot for an eye is often worthwhile. Of course, it is possible to paint with full details or use lines painted or burned on to indicate major parts. Animal cutouts look best if they are chunky, in reasonable approximation to size. If you cut them thin and you want them to stand, you will have to provide bases. Thin cutouts may be fixed to backgrounds as decorations.

Thinner cutouts could be plywood. Thick hardwood plywood looks effective with exposed veneer edges under a clear finish, but for most thicker animal cutouts it is better to use solid wood. For most animals it is best to choose close-grained hardwood. Some parts will usually be cross-grained, so softer or more open-grained wood might break.

Some outlines are suggested (FIGS. 2-3, 4 and 5). Note the effect of the addition of eyes to some examples. Reproduce to the size you want, using squares; al-

Fig. 2-3. Birds make attractive cutouts.

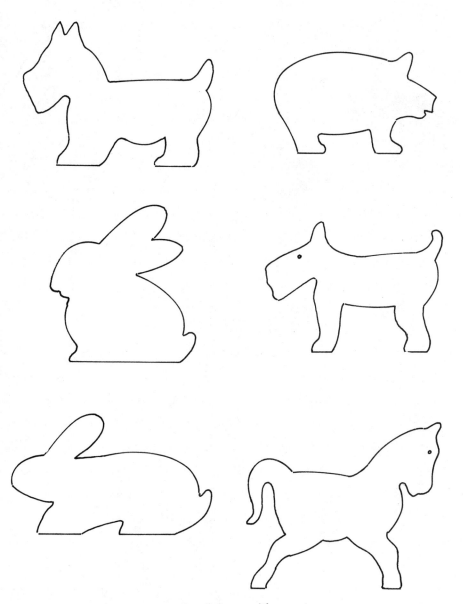

Fig. 2-4. Animal cutouts may be plain or with eyes.

though, you might try copying freehand. No two animals are alike, and slight variations from the original in your shape may not matter. If you copy pictures in books or elsewhere you may have to thicken thin parts, for strength. Where there are fine details, like feather ends, you will have to draw a sweeping curve with just a few token projections.

Fig. 2-5. More animal cutouts.

As a guide to wood thicknesses with your animal standing just on its edge, anything up to 3-inches long should be ½-inch thick. At 6 inches, it is better at ⅝-inch or ¾-inch thick, while bigger animals may be 1-inch thick.

Some animals, especially birds, have rather small flat bottoms if they are to be reasonably proportioned. You may wish to add a base to one of these; this would apply to any of the cutouts if you use thin wood.

Cut a thin wood base with straight edges, but use the scroll saw to make a more pleasing shape (FIG. 2-6A). Attach it with glue and screws from below. For a further refinement, glue a piece of cloth on the underside.

An alternative is to make a pair of feet with shallow notched joints into the bird (FIG. 2-6B). The feet may be the same thickness as the bird and arranged so the flat bottom of the cutout does not quite reach the surface; then the risk of rocking is reduced.

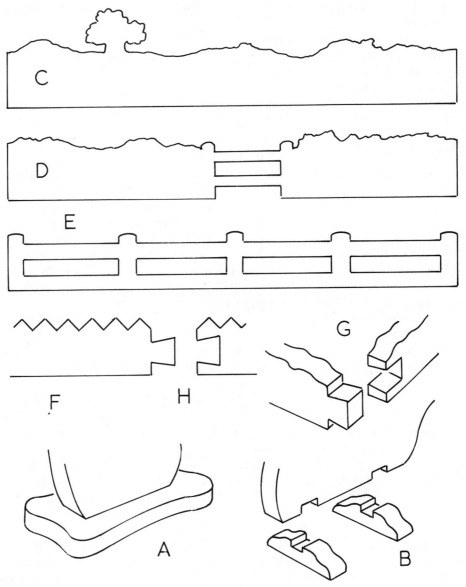

Fig. 2-6. Fences cut for use with animals may interlock.

If you make a set of animals and birds as toys for a child, he will welcome the means of forming a boundary to his farm or zoo. This may be assembled from strips, which can be put together in different ways, or you could choose to mount them on a hardboard or plywood base.

Cut outlines of bushes and trees (FIG. 2-6C) in any length. There might be an indication of a stile or gate (FIG. 2-6D). If you would rather have a rail fence, it cannot be to scale or the parts would be too fine, but you might symbolize the rails and posts (FIG. 2-6E). A picket fence could be indicated by a serrated top edge (FIG. 2-6F). Cut fence strips from wood thick enough to stand without much risk of pushing over.

Add interest to a fence made of sections by providing joints. So the pieces will match where they meet, arrange all ends the same height, even if there are variations further along. Use dovetails of the same size in the length and at corners; then it will be possible to vary the assembly.

Mark and cut a dovetail joint to suit a corner (FIG. 2-6G). Use the tail to mark other joints, so lengthwise parts will link in a similar way (FIG. 2-6H).

SOLID JIGSAW PUZZLES

With the ability of a scroll saw to cut through thick wood you can make jigsaw puzzles more solid than the usual sheet pictorial puzzles. A child will enjoy putting together an animal from a few chunky pieces of wood which lock together. The animal can then be treated as if it were one piece. Of course, it would be possible to divide the animal into a large number of pieces to make the puzzle more difficult. The appeal of fewer pieces will be mainly to a young child who will be happier to achieve results with simpler pieces, than be frustrated by something too complex.

The puzzles do not have to be animals or birds. Choose many other shapes that are familiar to a child. The size should be reasonable to handle, and the finished object should be thick enough to give a broad base for standing. It would be reasonable to use a length of about 6 inches and a thickness of 1 inch. A close-grained hardwood with the minimum of drawn or burned surface markings would be suitable for a child. If you want a display item, the puzzle could be made of a hardwood with an interesting grain and given a clear finish.

Some of the outlines given in FIG. 2-3, 4 and 5 could be enlarged to suit. Avoid thin projections, to reduce breakages. You may still use a basic shape by rounding such places. It is best to choose a pattern that is fairly deep in relation to its length, so jigsaw patterns can be quite large.

Mark and cut the chosen outline; then divide it with random cuts across. Arrange all parts so they interlock, and the finished animal will hold together. The Scottie dog is an example (FIG. 2-7). Some possible shapes are shown (FIGS. 2-8 and 9), with some non-animal shapes in FIG. 2-10, but you can adapt some of the other earlier patterns or find them in book illustrations.

Arrange cuts across boldly. In most cases, one interlocking loop in a cut should be sufficient. Avoid creating a very acute corner where you saw from an edge. Cut in square to an edge or at a fairly obtuse angle to it. The cutting lines

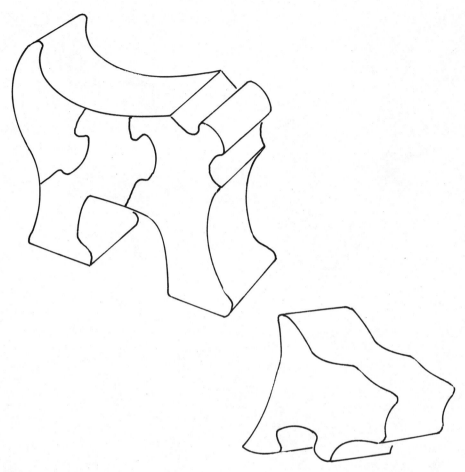

Fig. 2-7. A thick cutout animal might be made into a puzzle with interlocking parts.

shown are suggestions. Do not make very small pieces; instead, try to finish with all pictures about the same size.

THICKENED CUTOUTS

Flat cutout animals and other objects are attractive and serve many purposes, but they are simple profiles which do not look at their best except from the side. You can improve appearance as well as stability by gluing shaped pieces together. The most obvious example is a four-legged animal, which only has two legs in most simple profile shapes. Give it four legs by joining them to the sides.

For most animals you can follow something like its actual bone joints in making the overlap (FIG. 2-11A). Continue the overlaps to provide a good area for glue (FIG. 2-11B). Use wood the same thickness for all parts, or use a thinner wood

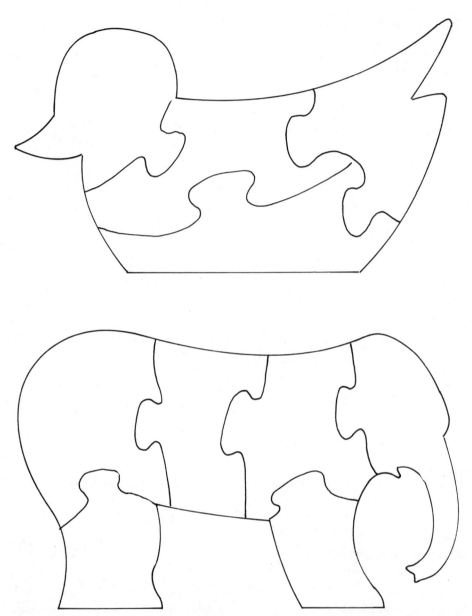

Fig. 2-8. Bird and elephant-thick jigsaw puzzles.

for the legs. Round the outer edges of the legs. If a good glue is used and the joints are clamped until the glue has set, there should be no need for pins or screws in the joints. Match opposite legs, but you might have to do a little planing of the bottoms to make the animal stand without wobbling.

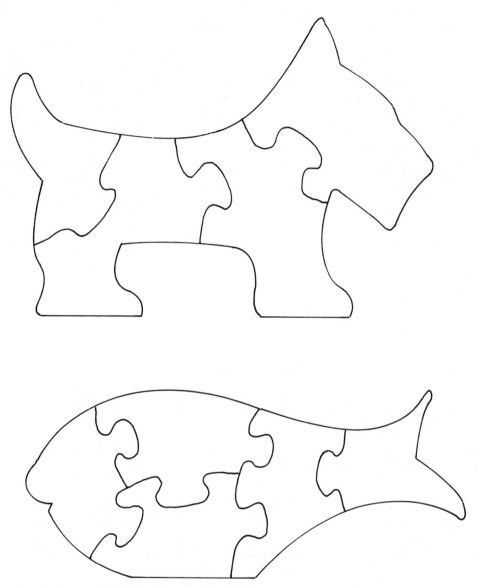

Fig. 2-9. *Dog and fish-thick jigsaw puzzles.*

Almost any four-legged animal may be treated in this way (Fig. 2-11C) including several of the cutouts already described. If there is much length to a leg, cut it with the grain lengthwise. This is particularly important with birds' slender legs.

Besides adding legs, you can thicken cutouts to give other effects. Keep the main part thick if it will have to provide a width of base for standing and make additions thinner.

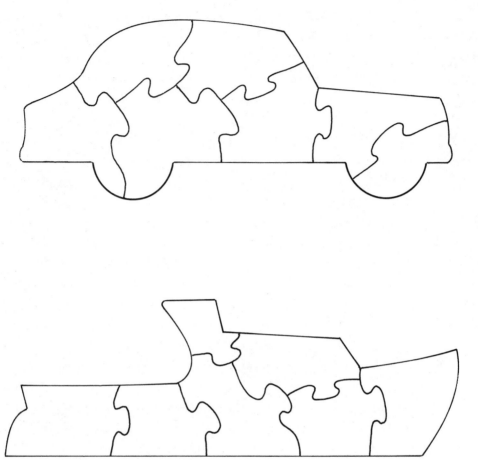

Fig. 2-10. Car and boat-thick jigsaw puzzles.

A tortoise, or other shelled creature, could have pieces added each side (FIG. 2-12A), so legs, head and tail appear to project. Use thinner wood for the added pieces and round their edges.

Add wings to a bird in the same way (FIG. 2-12B). In this case, the wings stand above the central body. Lightly round projecting edges before assembly.

The same techniques can be used for other projects. Wheels might be glued to each side of a cart. Sails may stand out from a windmill. Arms and legs may be on each side of a teddy bear. For animals with large ears, add ears as well as legs on each side.

JEWELRY AND DECORATIONS

Small pieces of material can be cut out and used to make such things as brooches, earrings, bracelets and decorations to be added to other assemblies. You can use thin wood, preferably with unusual or attractive grain. Some exotic woods are only available in small pieces. Also, use some of your accumulation of wood

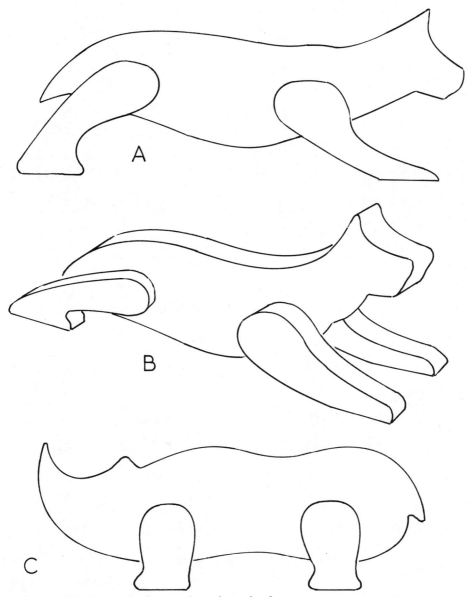

Fig. 2-11. Cutout animals may have legs glued on.

scraps from other work. Many types of thin solid plastic materials may be cut to make ornaments or decorations. Metal is the obvious choice for jewelry. Although gold and silver sheets might be cut with a scroll saw, the cost is prohibitive. Instead, make small decorative items from almost any sheet metal and it will look attractive when polished. Copper and its alloys look good when polished. Copper itself does not cut as well as its alloys of bronze and brass. Similarly, aluminum

Fig. 2-12. Tortoise and bird cutouts are made in three thicknesses.

does not cut as cleanly as its alloys. However, what is sold as aluminum is usually an alloy. Polished metal should be lacquered, or painted with a synthetic gloss.

Wood should not be more than ⅛-inch thick, which means softwood will not be strong enough, but many of the choice hardwoods can be cut into fairly intricate shapes without too much risk of breakage. Metal could be as thick as ⅛ inch, but most of what you cut will be thinner. Sheet metal thickness is known by its gauge number—the higher the number the thinner the metal. Most of what you use is likely to be between #12 gauge and #18 gauge. Metal with a higher number will be too flexible. If you regard #16 gauge as being about 1/16 inch, use it as an approximation to provide guidance.

You can obtain a large range of what are usually called *findings*; these are pins, rings, brooch fittings, ear clips and similar things for mounting jewelry. Some have lugs for pressing into softened plastics. Some may be drilled for tiny screws. Most are intended to be stuck on. Epoxy adhesives will join almost anything to anything else. The exceptions are a few plastics, but even then a glued joint may take the comparatively light load imposed by a piece of jewelry. You need a two-part epoxy adhesive. There is a resin and a hardener, both in tubes. Squeeze a little of each onto a board or card; then, mix them with a pointed stick. Instructions will indicate the setting time. It could be as much as three days for maximum strength, but you can handle the piece long before that. The longer the setting time, the stronger the joint, but even the quick-setting epoxy adhesives are strong enough for jewelry. If you have to remove surplus adhesive, wait until it is not quite hard; then it is easily picked off. When fully hardened, it is difficult to remove without damaging the surface.

If you intend to cut a small intricate outline from sheet metal, it is easier to polish the metal before cutting than to try to get an even shine on it after shaping, particularly if you use a powered polishing buff. This also applies to plastics, but with wood you apply the shine in the form of wax or other polish, which can often be done just as well after cutting.

It is difficult to draw fine detail directly on a surface, and it is better to have the pattern on paper which you stick on with an adhesive that will hold during cutting, but which can be peeled away afterwards. Rubber cement and some paper pastes are suitable.

Some of the cutout animals and letters already described could be reduced to make jewelry. For instance, an initial could make a pendant or a key ring and an animal on a suitable finding would form a brooch. More suggested shapes are on the following pages.

In general, you have a choice of providing a frame in which the motif is cut out or of letting the whole thing be the design. The elliptical pieces (FIG. 2-13A) are intended to have metal rings through the holes, so they can be used on neck chains or as earrings. Too much is cut away for there to be space behind for a brooch fitting. The cutout depends on a light or a colored background showing through to emphasize the design. Alternatively, you can cut the shape as the design itself (FIG. 2-13B) with little or no holes cut in the design. These could have brooch backs.

If you want to cut out a pattern and leave space for a brooch back, there must be enough solid material, preferably toward the top as in the heart designs (FIG. 2-13C), so the brooch fitting can be attached there and the whole brooch will not tend to fall forward.

For key rings you can be whimsical (FIG. 2-13D), or some names can be made into chunky pieces (FIG. 2-13E). Select letters that will not produce weak, short-grained or projecting parts.

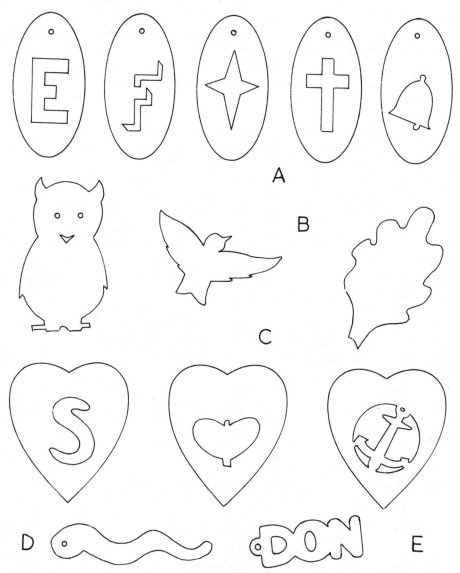

Fig. 2-13. Patterns for jewelry in wood, metal or plastics.

A further selection of possible designs is shown in FIG. 2-14. Sizes can vary. You may cut an earring in metal less than 1-inch across, while a brooch might be in plastic or thin wood up to 2-inches across. A decoration to apply to a surface might be even bigger, and they all come from the same design.

Some further possible variations are paper knives and buttons (FIG. 2-15), which are both decorative and useful. Metal, thin wood and plastic are all possible materials. Knives may be 4-inches to 6-inches long. Although buttons may be small, they are more decorative if comparatively large and in contrasting color to the material behind them, possibly ¾ inch to 1½-inches across.

A paper knife is intended to tear open envelopes rather than cut them, but the edges of the blade should be thinned. Leave the handle the full thickness, but either taper the blade section both ways (FIG. 2-15A) or give it an elliptical section (FIG. 2-15B). You can take metal to a thinner edge than you can wood or plastic.

Some earlier patterns could be adapted to knife handle shapes, but others are shown (FIG. 2-15C). You might include cutouts in the handle, but usually they should be just the basic outline (FIG. 2-15D). Handles could be personalized by

Fig. 2-14. More patterns for jewelry.

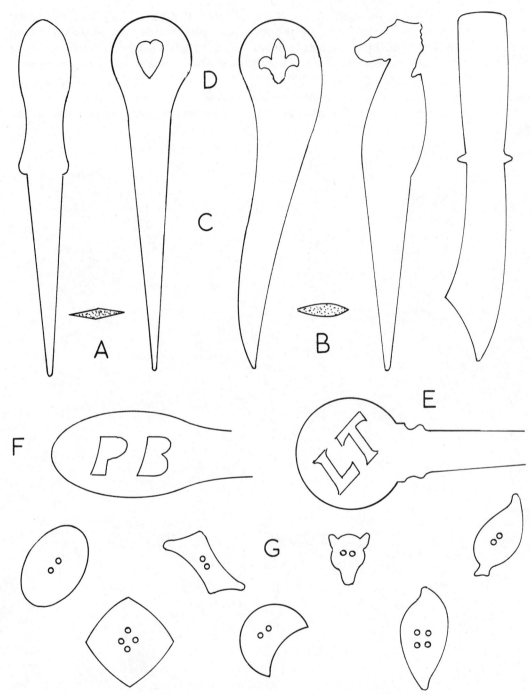

Fig. 2-15. Paper knives and buttons make small decorative items.

cutting initials (FIG. 2-15E). Characters will be too small for the centers of open letters to be included and held with bars, but they will be recognizable in outline only (FIG. 2-15F).

Buttons may be almost any shape, providing they will not pull back through buttonholes (FIG. 2-15G). There could be two or four small holes. Avoid very sharp or pointed outlines. If any part of the chosen design would normally be sharp, well round the points. You should also round edges at least enough to take off sharpness, so the button cannot catch in cloth. Very lightly countersink the holes on each side, so the risk of breaking the thread is reduced.

Three

Basic Flat Projects

One attraction of the scroll saw as a tool is that you can use it to make many things out of single pieces of wood. These articles are complete in themselves, so you do not have the problem of joints and making two or more parts to fit each other. This gives scope for using up odd pieces of wood and provides anyone new to scroll sawing with opportunities to make things in a short time. The results are there to see, usually with little effort.

With little wood involved, you can afford to take risks. If experiments with a project are not successful, you will not have lost much in time or money, but you will have learned by the experience. If you are new to using a scroll saw try making a few one-piece flat projects.

Try working with different materials and thicknesses. Plywood is a fairly universal scroll saw material, but many hardwoods are attractive and usually more suitable than softwoods. In fact, you can often achieve satisfying results with hardboard or particleboard.

If you want to make articles in quantity for sale or as gifts, flat projects are particularly suitable for consideration, as there is very little time-consuming extra work to be done.

HANGING BOARDS

A board with a row of hooks or pegs can have many uses. The Shakers put rows of pegs around a room and hung just about everything that was out of use on them. You might not want to go as far as that, but there are several places where a board with a few pegs or hooks can be useful. You can hang keys from small hooks and clothing from pegs or larger hooks. Although a plain piece of wood may make a backboard, with a scroll saw you can cut something less austere and more decorative, from the purely ornamental to something with a touch of whimsy.

There are screw hooks (or hook screws) available straight (FIG. 3-1A) or curved (FIG. 3-1B) in several sizes and metals. Some are coated with plastic. Any may be described as cup hooks. For our purpose, the better hooks have a bolster behind the screwed part (FIG. 3-1C). This gives a firmer hold as you drive the screw into a pre-drilled hole.

Buy or turn wooden Shaker pegs (FIG. 3-1D) for hanging clothing or other items too large for metal hooks. These are based on the Shaker originals and are available in several sizes. The end dowels glue into holes. An alternative is to use a piece of dowel rod, preferably tilted (FIG. 3-1E). It should be sufficiently strong to merely glue the peg into the hole, but if you need extra strength, it can be wedged from the back. Make a saw cut in the end of the peg before inserting it, with the cut across the grain of the backboard; then, drive in a small glued wedge (FIG. 3-1F). Plane level after the glue has set.

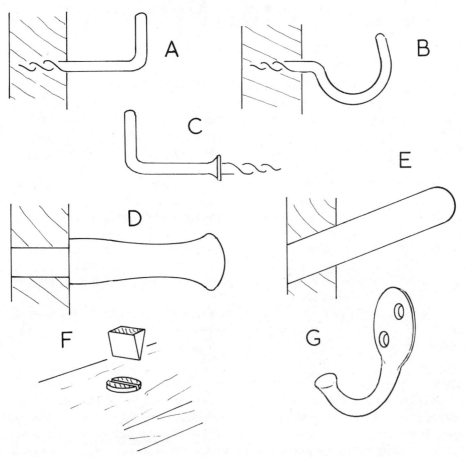

Fig. 3-1. Hooks and pegs of several types may be needed on hanging boards.

There are many types of coat hooks, but as an alternative to pegs, a simple type held by two screws is suitable (FIG. 3-1G). For double hooks, make a larger board. Mix the types of hook or peg on a board to suit your needs. For instance, you might desire different hooks on a board inside the back door to take a couple of keys, the dog's lead and an umbrella. In a kitchen, you might want to hang a row of mugs alongside a key, a handle for the grill, and your oven gloves.

Key boards offer plenty of variety in scroll saw work. You could make a board with quite ornate fretwork and spaces for a few hooks, but the most popular key boards, particularly if you are making boards to sell, are those which are simpler and indicate their purpose.

A key board should be thick enough to take the screwed parts of the hooks, which usually means ½ inch, although you might be able to reduce to ⅜ inch. However, with some designs you also have to consider the amount of short grain in some parts, which will be less liable to break if the wood is thick. Once the board is attached to the wall, there would be little risk of short grain damage.

Key boards look well if made of an attractive close-grained hardwood that has been given a clear finish, but you could use plywood and paint it.

Four possible shapes are suggested, drawn on squares that will give 9-inch finished lengths, but vary this by using squares of different sizes when you transfer to the wood. No holes for screws to the wall are shown, but they may come near the ends or between the end hook positions.

Outlines of keys are popular (FIG. 3-2A and B). The only vulnerable piece of short grain is in a part of the first key (FIG. 3-2C), but widen or alter the shape there if you think your wood may be too weak.

The word *keys* will make the use of the rack obvious. A shape with a bar across the letters (FIG. 3-3A) results in very little short grain, so almost any wood could be used. The letters on the other rack (FIG. 3-3B) would be safe in plywood, but otherwise you should choose a strong hardwood.

If the letters are enclosed (FIG. 3-4) the problem of short grain is negligible; use almost any wood for this key board. The board might be cut with all edges square, but you could tilt the saw table to give a beveled edge around the outline. Hang the board with screws through the two holes indicated near the top.

Pegs or larger hooks for hanging clothing might be mounted on a straight board, but with a scroll saw you can provide a shaped outline. Although a scroll saw will cut them, straight edges are more easily made by other means. You could make an elaborate shape, possibly with many cutouts, but a peg board for hanging clothing is mostly hidden and your detailed work might not be appreciated.

For most purposes, the decoration might be limited to wavy edges (FIG. 3-5A). This gives an interesting appearance and breaks up an otherwise austere look. Make the edge cuts with the saw table tilted to give a beveled border.

The lower part of a board with pegs or coat hooks is mostly hidden in use by hanging clothes, so any additional decoration should be at the top. For children's use, you might add birds, animals, flowers or outlines of family pets (FIG. 3-5B).

You could cut the whole board in the form of an animal, bird or fish, providing there is space to arrange sufficient hooks or pegs. Much depends on the

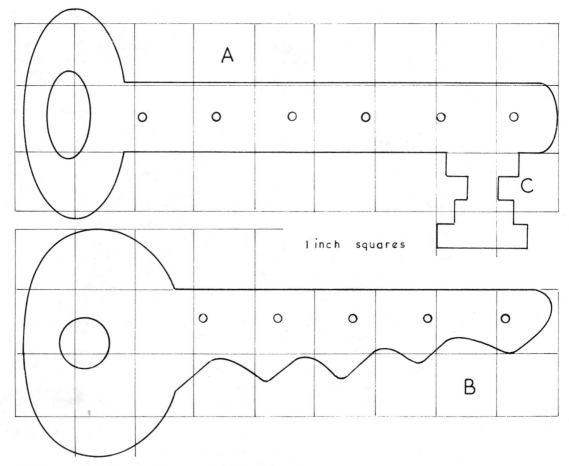

Fig. 3-2. Key racks may be in the shape of keys.

situation. A fancy shape may not be acceptable in formal surroundings, although it may suit a playroom. One type of shape suitable for use almost anywhere is a formalized outline of a leaf (FIG. 3-6A and B).

If you will be using Shaker pegs or dowels, allow sufficient thickness to take the loads. Do not have peg holes too close to edges. Let there be solid wood, at least as wide as the diameter of a peg. Coat hooks should be kept a reasonable distance from the edges, for the sake of appearance as well as strength.

DOOR PLATES

Give your doors an individual stamp by making your own finger plates for pushing doors open, or number plates. You might even consider putting names or symbols on the doors of particular rooms.

I inch squares

Fig. 3-3. Words indicate the purpose of a rack.

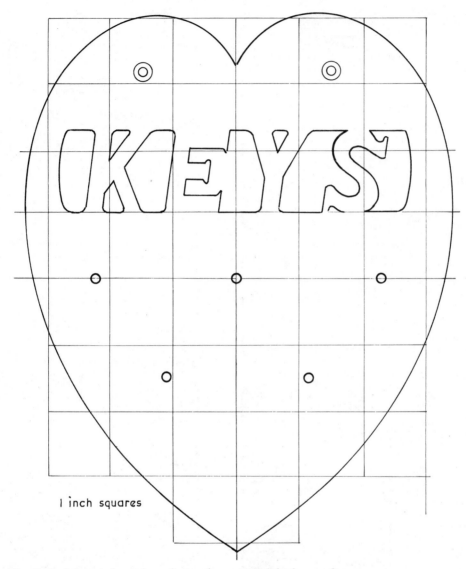

I inch squares

Fig. 3-4. A heart shape is a change from a straight key rack.

Finger plates are there to prevent the door surfaces from becoming soiled through constant use, so your plates must be able to withstand heavy use. They need not be thicker than ¼ inch, but could be made from hardwood with interesting grain patterns that will show through a hard transparent gloss finish. They could be painted, if that suits your decor, but scroll-sawn wood in its natural color will be good examples of your craftsmanship, to be admired by all who appreciate this individual touch in your home.

A reasonable overall size is 3 inches ×9 inches (FIG. 3-7A), but check on what size would be most suitable for your particular situation. Ends may be cut to a

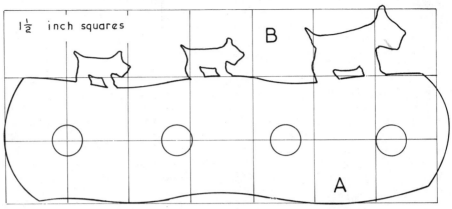

$1\frac{1}{2}$ inch squares

B

A

Fig. 3-5. Animal cutouts can decorate a pegged rack for clothing.

formal architectural shape (FIG. 3-7B). Bought finger plates would have identical patterns on both ends, but the plate looks better if the bottom pattern matches the top, although deeper (FIG. 3-7C). Two central screw holes are suggested, but if you want to make sure the wood stays flat, you could have four holes, arranged near the corners of the wide part.

You might include a number in the plate. It would be difficult to have a cutout number with several figures of a worthwhile size in an upright plate, but a single number would be sufficiently prominent (FIG. 3-7D). Any outside shape might be used, but something simple would not detract from the number, which should be easily recognizable.

You can draw the shapes of cutout numbers in many styles. There are examples of freehand numbers and letters in different forms elsewhere in this book, but if you are not artistic and do not trust your ability to draw the shapes you require, there is a basic way of producing acceptable outlines for piercing, as required in the examples in this project.

The outlines are based on a pattern of squares, three wide and five high (FIG. 3-8A). Choose the square size to suit your needs. The straight parts of numbers fit on the lines of the grid; except, the upright part of a 4 is moved over half a space. Number 1 is only one square wide. The curved parts of numbers are circles drawn to fit in the grid. Numbers 2, 3, 5, and 7 are simple to draw in this way (FIG. 3-8B).

The other numbers have centers that would fall out if cut completely, so narrow bars have to be included to hold them. There is more than one way of arranging the bars for some numbers, but recommended ways are shown. For 0, 4 and 8 there can be two bars (FIG. 3-8C), so these may be fairly narrow. With 6 and 9 it is neatest to have single bars (FIG. 3-8D), so they should be wider, for strength.

If you pierce these shapes so they are supported at the top and bottom by surrounding wood, there should be ample strength, particularly when the cutout wood is attached to a solid backing. If the backing is a contrasting color, the numbers will look attractive and they can be easily read. If it is a number on a

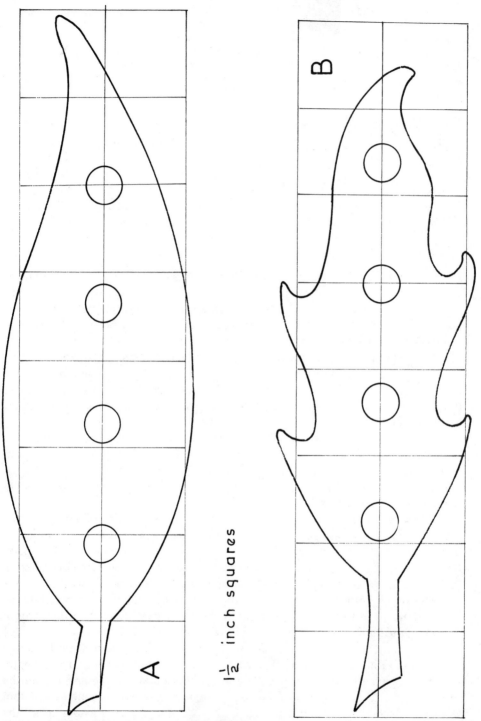

Fig. 3-6. *These patterns use leaves as rack outlines.*

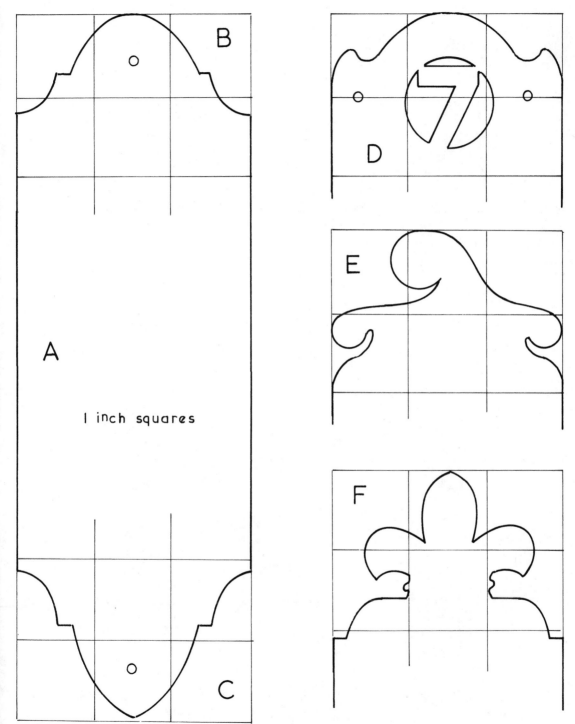

B

A

1 inch squares

C

D

E

F

Fig. 3-7. Door plates may be parallel with decorated ends.

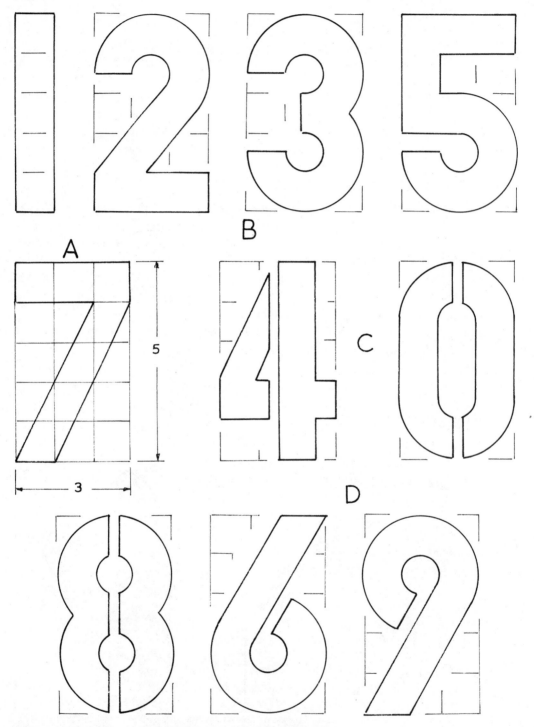

Fig. 3-8. Plain figures may be based on patterns of squares.

door, you want visitors to be able to read it correctly and easily, so these simple outlines are a good choice.

The ends of a door plate may be shaped in many different ways. Avoid very thin parts, particularly if cross-grained. Use a stylized pattern (FIG. 3-7E), or incorporate a badge or emblem (FIG. 3-7F).

Demonstrate your skill with a fine blade by using a design with cutouts (FIG. 3-9A) or cut leaf shapes (FIG. 3-9B). In these cases, the bottom could be worked the same or left in a rather plainer or simplified form. It is the top of an upright piece, at or below eye level, that gets attention.

Similar plates may be used horizontally. Make a long plate with a plain center on which the name or number can be painted. Add cutout letters glued on, as described later in the book, but here we are concerned with numbers cut in the single thickness of wood. The length of the plate will have to be made to incorporate the number of digits in your number.

Work from the numbers outwards in designing your plate. Draw the numbers and arrange the supporting shape around them; then, complete the outside pattern, which could be any of the designs intended for finger plates. One simple outline is suggested (FIG. 3-9C).

Although a mainly parallel shape is usually preferable for a finger plate, you are not so restricted in the choice of outline for a number plate, and you can avoid straight lines completely (FIG. 3-9D). If there is sufficient space on the door, you might choose a most ornate fretted design, or cut the outline of an animal or bird.

LETTERED SIGNS

Name and number boards can be made by piercing, as just described, but for many purposes it is better to cut out the characters and mount them on a backboard. It might be plain or ornate, or it may be the actual door or wall. The cutting of individual letters and numbers for mounting in this way could form a large part of the work of a user of a scroll saw.

You have only to study the make-up of a newspaper or magazine to see that there is an infinite variety of print styles, and most of them are suitable for cutting in wood with a scroll saw. For our purposes use letters of fairly plain outline that will be easy to cut and read; hence, the more fanciful outlines should be avoided. For such things as house names, you will usually only consider capital letters. Capitals and small letters used together are not often pleasing on such a sign, but there are exceptions. Print type will give you plenty of ideas for letter shapes, and you may develop cut styles that appeal to you. However, in the first instance it is wiser to concentrate on block letters with few flourishes or decorations. A suitable alphabet is suggested (FIGS. 3-11, 12 and 13). For early efforts large sizes are advised, at least 3 inches high, but the same outlines can be used for smaller names.

Design letters in the same 3 × 5 grid as suggested for cutout figures, but a few letters, such as M and W, are better made wider. This applies to most letter patterns.

Letters may be upright or sloping. If you choose to slope keep the angle slight —between 5 degrees and 10 degrees to vertical is sufficient (FIG. 3-10A). Cut a piece

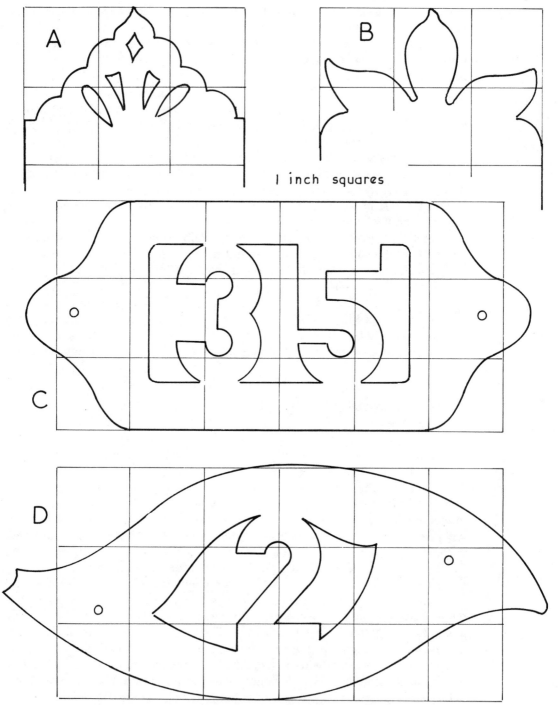

I inch squares

Fig. 3-9. Door plates may be decorated or include a number.

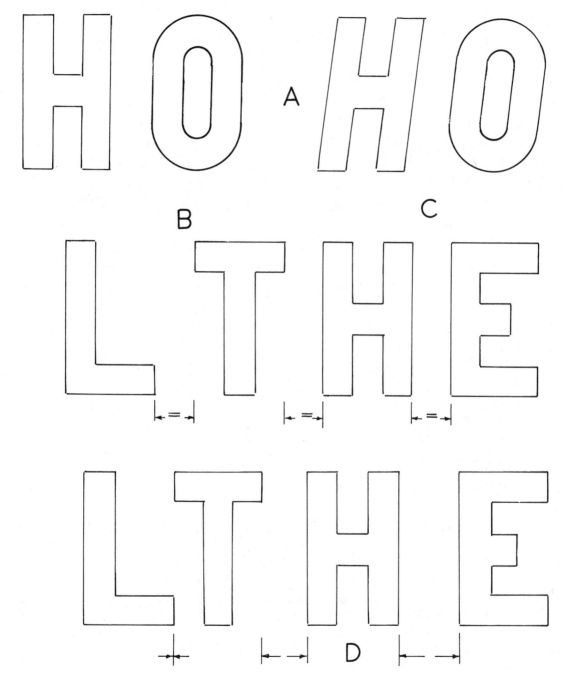

Fig. 3-10. Letters may be upright or sloping; spacing is better with equal areas than with uniform horizontal spacing.

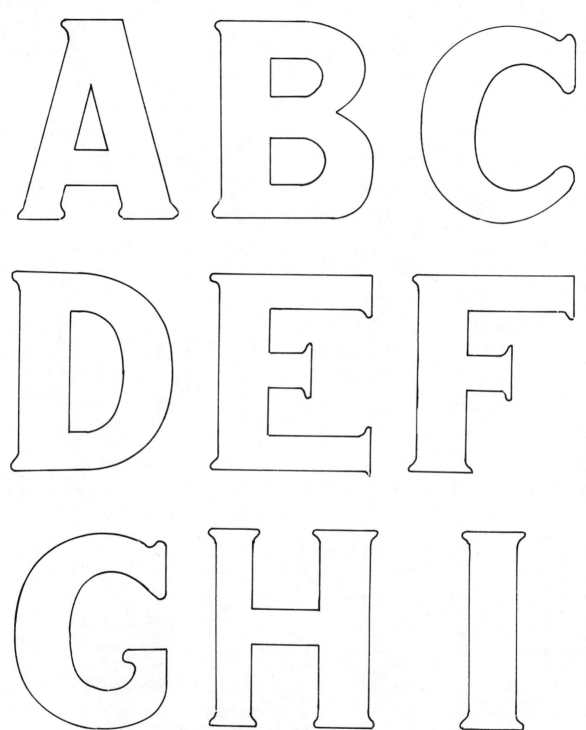

Fig. 3-11. Patterns for letters using varying widths.

Fig. 3-12. More letters. Note that M has to be wider.

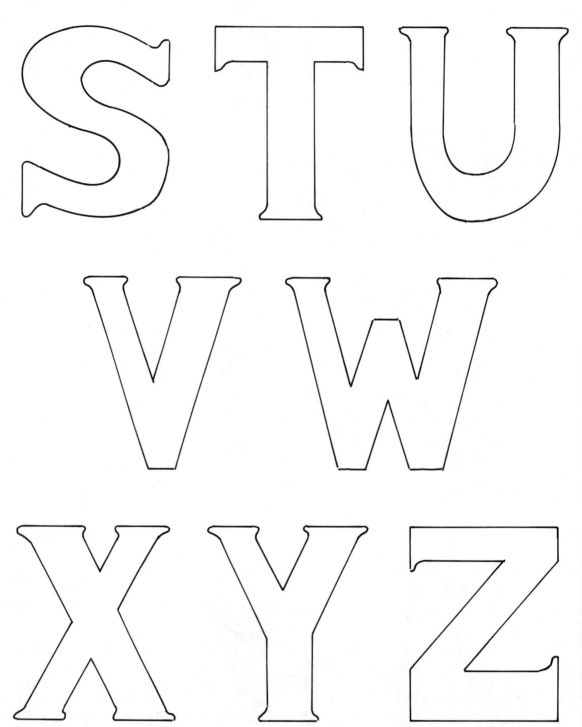

Fig. 3-13. More letters, with W drawn wider.

of hardboard to the angle to horizontal and use it as a template when drawing the letters and mounting them.

For a sign with applied letters, it is advisable to decide on an approximate overall size, but leave final trimming to exact size until you have cut the letters and tried laying them out for a pleasing appearance.

Thicknesses of wood are important. A thick letter casts more shadow and is therefore more prominent than a thin one, but if letters are so close that shadows go over onto a next letter, distinctions begin to blur. Spacing is also important. Do not mark out exact divisions without considering the letters. If you do that, the whole assembly of letters may look uneven. For instance, the gap between L and T (FIG. 3-10B) might look wider than the gap between two squarer letters (FIG. 3-10C), although the horizontal spacing is the same. Arrange areas of space between letters about the same to get a neat appearance (FIG. 3-10D).

Mount cutout letters with a straightedge and square discrepancies in the alignment of a word will be very obvious to a viewer. If you use a sloping type, check that all letters are at the same angle, as well as being in line and spaced with gaps of equal area.

An interesting alternative to mounting cutout letters takes advantage of the ability of a scroll saw to cut at a constant angle if the sawing table is tilted. You can tilt the cut so the amount removed by the saw allows you to push the letter outwards (FIG. 3-14A). Judge the amount of slope so the top edge of the cut border is slightly less than the bottom edge of the cut letter (FIG. 3-14B); therefore, the letter may be pushed almost through. Experiment with the chosen saw blade to get the correct penetration. If it is glued in that position, you have the effect of a letter put on the surface, although the backboard and the letter are made from the same piece of wood. If it is a letter with an unattached center, that can be pushed back (FIG. 3-14C). Obviously, you must arrange the final word, so that all letters are level and project the same amount.

How you make the backboard for your sign depends on several factors. If it is to be attached to a door or wall, it may be comparatively thin. If it has to stand away from such a background it should be thick enough to hold its shape and look solid. If it is a long name, you may choose a parallel board with any decoration at

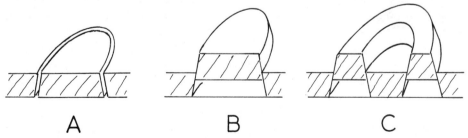

A   B   C

Fig. 3-14. By using a sloping cut, letters and other shapes can be made by raising part of the backboard.

the ends only. If there are two words, one above the other, there could be all around decoration. The name might suggest an outline for the board — *The Forge* could be on an anvil, *The Nest* might have a bird outline, and *The Moorings* might be a ship. In some circumstances, the backboard could be a large arrow.

A long parallel board to be screwed to something else might have an architectural design at each end (FIG. 3-15A), for example, you could have an asymmetrical end (FIG. 3-15B and C). In those cases, invert the design at the other end. Simulate a log with an apparently torn end and wavy edges instead of straight parallel ones (FIG. 3-15D). Use some formalized leaves (FIG. 3-15E) or flowers. The log or leaves idea might even have some connection with the name.

If you want to use the scroll saw more extensively, particularly on a wider board for a name at two levels, shape all the outline (FIG. 3-15F). Carried a stage further, make some internal cuts (FIG. 3-15G). However, elaborate fretting is inappropriate, and it might detract from the name, which is the focal point of the assembly.

The letters can be mounted in several ways; it is important that they finish level and upright. Glue alone might be sufficient, but it is then difficult to align the letters and keep them in position. You could drive two fine pins in each letter, then punch them below the surface and cover them with stopping. Another way would be to use two fine screws to each letter, driven through the back into the letter; that would be strong and the fastenings would not show on the surface.

If the letters and backboard are to have the same finish, as when they are of contrasting woods and require a clear treatment, assemble the sign completely. When the letters are to be a different color from the backboard, do all painting before assembly, and allow ample time for the paint to dry. Allow for the backboard support, and drill for screws that will hold it to a post or wall before painting.

NOTE AND BULLETIN BOARDS

There are always needs for note pads in the kitchen and den, as well as by the telephone and elsewhere in the house. If the note pad is glued to a backing board that can be hung on a nail, it is unlikely to be lost. If pads are needed for different purposes or by different people, names can be cut into the board.

Similarly, there are needs for bulletin or notice boards, where reminders, programs and anything else to be noted can be displayed. Besides their use in the home, bulletin boards are needed in club rooms, churches and other meeting places.

With a scroll saw, you can make these boards in a way that is unique. No one else will have a board like the one you make — unless you make a quantity for sale.

For a note pad, you will have to arrange sizes to suit available tear-off paper pads (FIG. 3-16A). Allow a border around the pad and enough above it for your cutout work and a hole for hanging (FIG. 3-16B). Hardwood plywood up to ¼-inch thick would be suitable. Consider using dense hardboard, particularly if the board

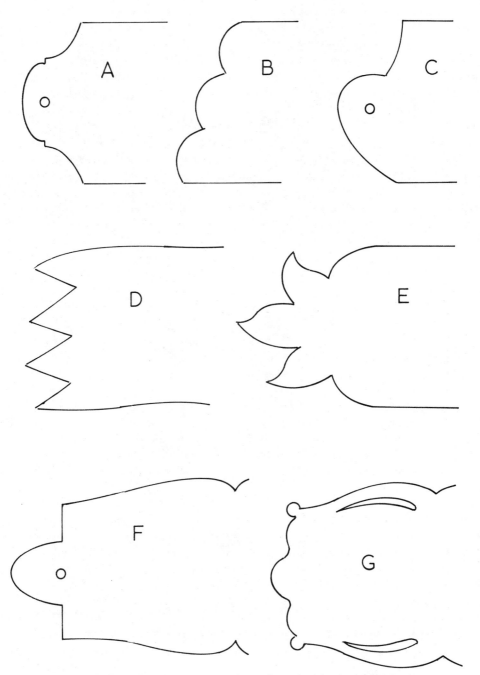

Fig. 3-15. Boards for mounting names and numbers may be decorated in many ways.

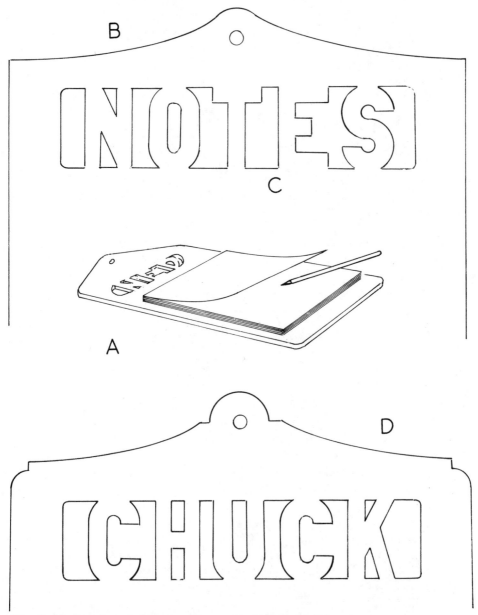

Fig. 3-16. Boards to hold note pads can be decorated with cutout names.

is not intended for a long life. Of course, you can glue on replacement pads many times on a durable board.

Use standard letters (FIG. 3-16C) or freehand ones in your own style. Sizes of letters will have to be adjusted to suit the pad and board. Avoid long names or titles, as a large number of letters would mean they have to be too small. Abbreviated names are suitable (FIG. 3-16D). Use your imagination. The word GET would suit a shopping list. COOK would show which board belonged to the kitchen. PHONE would indicate the one to be kept by the telephone.

A bulletin board can be as large as you wish. It is best made to be hung from two nails or hooks (FIG. 3-17A). If papers are to be held by adhesive tape, it does not matter if the board is hard. If you want to use thumb tacks, face the board with a softer material; this could be thin cork. On a large board, it could be softboard. If you paint a narrow border on the soft material, that will reduce the risk of crumbling as well as improve appearance.

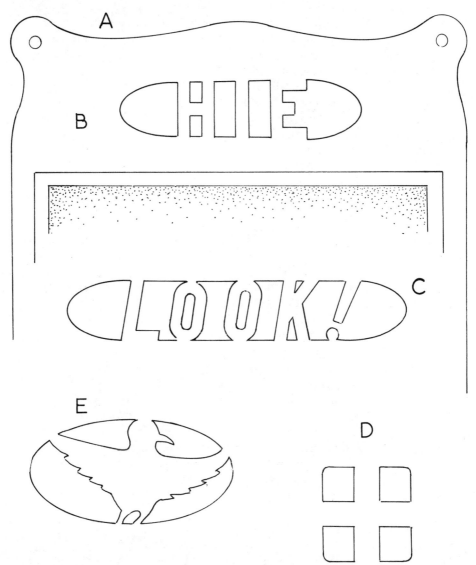

Fig. 3-17. A bulletin board can have a cutout title or emblem.

The thickness of plywood depends on the size of the board. Lettering shows best if it is proportional to the thickness of the wood. If you use ½-inch plywood, lettering looks better if it is larger than you use on ¼-inch plywood.

As with the note pads, shorter names are better than long ones. You could use the obvious NOTICES, but there is room for more individual words (FIG. 3-17B and C).

If the board is for a church or club, you might include the name or initials. Plain letters always show clearly, but you could use fancy designs. Avoid excessive flourishes, which may be difficult to cut and could be confusing to read.

If the organization has an emblem or badge you could cut that, but there are restrictions. Cut only an outline, which may have to be simplified if there are fine edge details in the badge. It is unlikely you will be able to cut internal details. Nothing could be simpler than the Red Cross emblem (FIG. 3-17D), but a bird or animal might have to be simplified (FIG. 3-17E).

If the board hangs on a wall of a color that contrasts with the wood, the lettering will show prominently. On a dark wall, you might consider painting the board a light color. An alternative, which means the color on the wall does not matter, is to back the cutout lettering with cloth of a contrasting color glued on, or use colored cardboard.

You can expand the idea to other things. These hardwood plywood place mats could be cut near an edge with individual names. Storage boxes could be cut on the side or lid with the name of the contents or the owner. In addition, a cutout panel might be glued on. Divisions between files or other contents of a drawer could have cutout names or numbers near projecting edges.

INLAID PANEL

With a scroll saw you can cut inlaid parts so they fit exactly, particularly if you work with thick veneer or even wood up to about ¼-inch thick. If the result is mounted on a plywood or other backing, the effect is as good as may be seen on antique furniture, done with considerable care and time by a medieval expert.

If you cut two thicknesses of thin wood with a scroll saw blade set squarely, the parts will match, except for the kerf (groove sawblade) removed, which will be the same as the thickness of the blade (FIG. 3-18A). With a very fine blade and woods of contrasting colors, this may not matter; you have the makings of a dark inlay in a light ground, or a light inlay in a dark ground (FIG. 3-18B).

For a close fit tilt the saw just enough to allow for the waste removed; then, the top of the lower inner piece will match the top of the upper outer piece (FIG. 3-18C) and it can be inserted from below with no gaps showing on the face (FIG. 3-18D). Of course, this only provides one inlay; trying to fit the waste from the top piece into the surround of the lower piece would result in a double width gap all around.

The method can be used where pieces have to be let into a larger piece to form a pattern. The pieces let in need not all be the same wood because you can put the appropriate wood under for cutting where it is needed. An easily peeled off

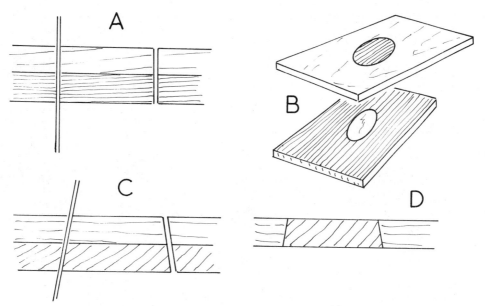

Fig. 3-18. An inlaid panel can be made by cutting two thicknesses at one time.

adhesive or paste that will grip temporarily can hold the parts being cut. It would be possible to cut pieces for a marquetry or inlaid picture in this way, but the method is particularly appropriate where pieces fit separately into holes without meeting each other, as in the example (FIG. 3-19).

The pattern can be adapted to various sizes, depending on the squares in your grid. Using 1-inch squares, the panel would be 12 inches × 16 inches. Use ¾ inch, ½ inch or any other size squares to suit your needs. If it is a door or tray of fixed size, trim the edges to get the right proportion.

The inlays should contrast with the main background. If that is dark, the flower parts may be a light color wood and the stems and leaves a moderate brown.

Use any woods between ³⁄₃₂-inch veneers to ¼-inch solid wood. Cut the main panel to size and mark out the pattern on it. Allow pieces below large enough for the inlays, but there need not be very much waste.

If grain markings are prominent, leaves and stems will look best with the grain the long way in each part. Otherwise, put a piece large enough under a stem and its leaves; then, cut them all at once.

When all parts are cut, put the panel face down on a clean flat surface and insert the inlay parts. Have the plywood backing ready. It may be slightly too large, set for trimming later. Glue it on under weights or other pressure. The finished front surface should be reasonably level, but you will probably have to sand it carefully. If the panel is to form part of a door, tray or other piece of furniture you can now treat it as a normal piece of wood and build it in. If you

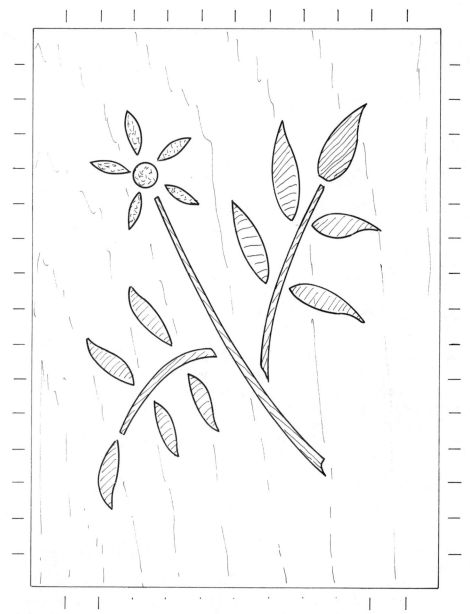

Fig. 3-19. A pattern for an inlaid panel using two types of wood.

want the panel to be a display item on its own, you can frame it in several ways. Simplest is to use picture frame molding directly and treat it as a picture, but it is possible to further show your skill with the scroll saw.

Inlay a border in a contrasting wood (FIG. 3-20A) either in one piece or four mitered strips. Use the same angled cutting technique, pushing the border close as

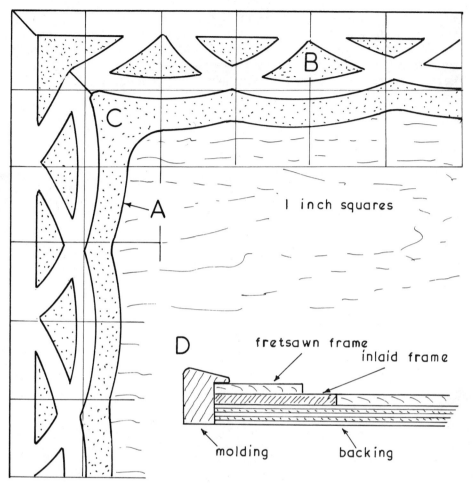

Fig. 3-20. *The inlaid panel may have an inlaid border, covered by a fretted frame; this can be surrounded by picture frame molding.*

it is glued. This may be all you need to display the panel in a frame, or as part of a piece of furniture.

With the inlaid border or in place of it, you can put a fretted border over the panel. It could be a most intricate piece of fretwork, but you want the central pictorial inlay to be the main feature, not the border. Therefore, a fairly simple pattern might be better. The pattern suggested (FIG. 3-20B) has some interweaving bands. Cut it in wood ⅛-inch thick, or even less. Do not try to cut the whole frame in one piece. Make four mitered sides. If there is an inlaid border, the fretted border outline should usually be parallel to it. You can stack opposite sides for piercing.

Arrange the units of the border to fit into the lengths of the sides. If the panel is 12 inches ×16 inches, as suggested, units have to be 2 inches or 4 inches, because they have to fit both directions. If you make a panel a different size you will have to find a divisor that allows you to fit in matching patterns both ways.

Use the pattern for a corner (FIG. 3-20C) and draw the four corners with linking patterns, marked by overlapping the design. Glue the border pieces in place with the minimum of glue, so you do not have an excess to clear out of awkward spaces. Finally, enclose the assembly in picture frame molding (FIG. 3-20D).

Four

Small Toys

A great many small toys include a large number of curved parts, so a scroll saw is particularly useful in making toys for your own or other people's children. They may also be a popular selling line. Many attractive toys are comparatively small, so they do not use much wood, and they are well within the scope of any scroll saw.

Wood used and any paint applied should be safe for use by a child. There should be little risk of splintering. Parts may find their way into a child's mouth. Use close-grained hardwoods for most toys. Avoid exposed edges of softwood plywood when possible. Avoid resinous or oily wood. Check that paint or other finishes will not harm a child who bites or sucks them.

If you use nails, countersink them below the surface and cover them with wood filler wherever possible. If there are hinges, hooks or other metal fittings, make sure there are no sharp or rough parts. Plastic attachments are probably safe, but avoid fragile or brittle pieces.

Many toys require wheels. There are many plastic and metal wheels available, but for smaller toys it might be better to use wooden wheels, which can be bought or made. If you have a lathe you can turn them, or you may cut slices of thick dowel rod.

An advantage of wooden wheels is that they can be glued to a dowel rod axle, which rotates with them. It may be sufficient to pass the axle through a hole in the bottom of a thick or low toy (FIG. 4-1A). If you want a greater spread for stability, you might add spacers, made by drilling pieces of dowel rod (FIG. 4-1B). All holes should be an easy fit on the axle, so it revolves easily. Candle wax on the dowel rod will provide lubrication.

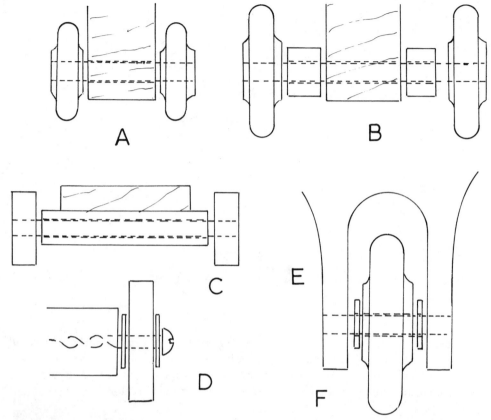

Fig. 4-1. Small wheeled toys can have wood or metal axles, or a wheel can be mounted on a screw.

You could run a wooden axle through a longer square piece of wood in a wider construction (FIG. 4-1C), but in many toys it might be better to pivot the wheels on screws. The gauge of a screw should suit the hole in the wheel, which will be settled if it is bought. If you are drilling your own wheels, #10 gauge screws through ³⁄₁₆-inch holes will suit many small toys. A screw should be long enough for the wheel to run on the plain neck of the screw, as far as possible, allowing for a washer on each side of the wheel (FIG. 4-1D). Roundhead screws look better and are safer in small hands.

In some toys you have to provide a single wheel. In fitting a wheel in notched wood, allow for a washer each side of the wheel, with just enough clearance for it to turn (FIG. 4-1E). Do not trim the wood ends too close to the axle. It is better to let them extend, to give strength in the end grain (FIG. 4-1F).

PULL-ALONG TOYS

A large variety of toys can be made that a child may pull along, either by sliding or on wheels, with handles or cords. Sizes may vary to suit the child, but most can be made from small pieces of wood. The toy may be an individual item, or it could consist of several items linked together.

Many of the animal cutouts described in Chapter 2 might have wheels added if made to a suitable size. Drawing a pattern to 6-inches long, and cutting from wood ¾-inch thick would be a suitable average to consider.

With some animal or bird patterns, you can use the base as it is and drill through for axles (FIG. 4-2A). This might be possible through some wider legs, but the toy will be stronger if you cut a base in the same wood, making it deep enough to take the axle holes. It could have a wavy top to stimulate the ground (FIG. 4-2B).

If an animal has much height in relation to its base, extended wheels (FIG. 4-1B) might give it enough stability, but it will probably be better to mount the animal on a broader platform base (FIG. 4-2C). Screw upwards into the legs or body.

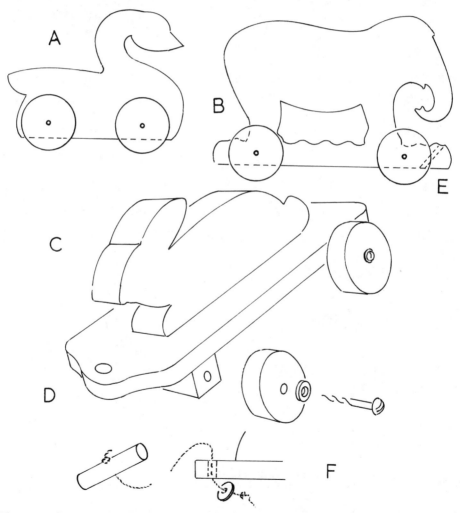

Fig. 4-2. Cutout animals on wheels make pull-along toys.

Fig. 4-3. Suggested shapes for cutout pull-along toys.

Provide a hole for the pulling cord (FIG. 4-2D and E). A piece of dowel rod will make a handle; it is a good idea to put a small washer or button on the knotted lower end to prevent if from pulling through (FIG. 4-2F).

You could produce some original designs by putting two or more animals on one base, possibly in two sizes. For example, you could make a mare and a foal, or you could position two different animals with a slight overlap.

Although a child may be happy with simple one color cutouts, you may prefer to paint with more detail and make any base green or brown to represent the ground.

Other cutouts on wheels might be based on vehicles of many sorts. Sizes may be up to 6-inches long, cut from wood ¾ inch or 1-inch thick. Wheels may be 1 inch in diameter and axles ¼-inch dowel rods. There can be several outlines of cars, with vans of various proportions, semi-trailers and such things as tractors and airplanes (FIG. 4-3). Keep to bold outlines that indicate what the shape is meant to

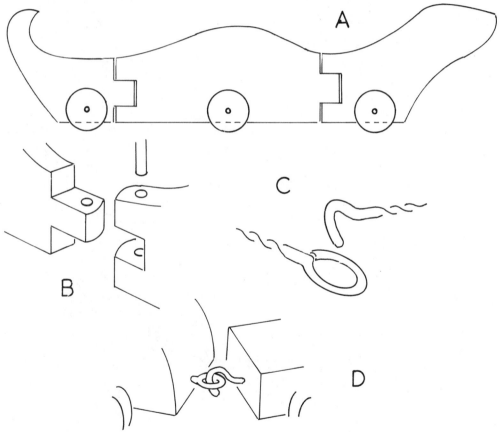

Fig. 4-4. An animal toy may be hinged and other toys can be hooked together.

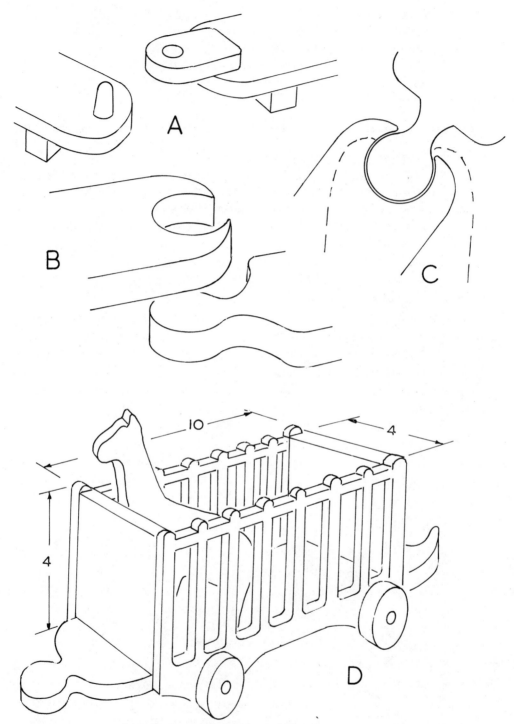

Fig. 4-5. *Joints between toys can be cut in the wood.*

be, but avoid very fine details. Some of these models are effective without much detailed paintwork or marking. The young user might not even notice what you add on the surface when he has identified the model by its shape.

Several wheeled parts may be linked together, either permanently or in a take apart assembly for the child.

A snake or other long animal might have vertical pivots and a pair of wheels on each section, so there are sideways movements as the toy is pulled along (FIG. 4-4A). The joint may be an 1/8-inch or 3/16-inch dowel through loosely fitted parts (FIG. 4-4B). On some animals, you may need four wheels on the front section, but in most cases two will be enough.

Use screw hooks and eyes (FIG. 4-4C). Make sure these are long enough for the thread to get a good grip, so a child is unlikely to pull them out. Join a cutout trailer to a car in this way (FIG. 4-4D), or link the wagons of a train.

If the wheeled sections have platform bases, there could be a pin on one piece and a matching socket on the other. Make the pin from a dowel rod, but taper it for easy fitting, and let the hole in the other part be an easy fit (FIG. 4-5A).

Another method of linking uses a similar sort of rounded dovetail to that used for interlocking cuts across a jigsaw puzzle (FIG. 4-5B). The projecting part must be part of a circle and its mating piece cut as part of an only slightly larger circle. Cut back the outer parts to give some sideways movement (FIG. 4-5C). This works best with fairly thick wood, as thin parts might jump apart during the rough use a child gives the toy.

You can make a set of wagons or trucks which link. They might be simple boxes to carry any small toys or they could be cattle transporters or a circus train. A typical wagon (FIG. 4-5D) has a solid wood base with the linking arrangements. There are 1/2-inch solid wood ends on it and pierced plywood sides attached. They extend down with holes to take the axles (FIG. 4-6). Sizes will have to be adjusted to suit animals of exceptional dimensions.

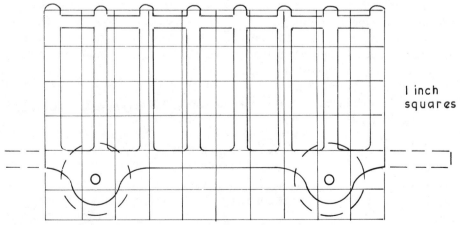

1 inch squares

Fig. 4-6. Sizes of a pull-along cage for cutout animals.

DOLL HOUSE FURNITURE

You can make most furniture needed in a doll house with a scroll saw, but it is important to plan your approach, so you produce a set of furniture that will look right and be in the correct proportions. You also have to decide how detailed you make each piece. For a young child it is more important to concentrate on strength than exact scale details. Even an older girl may be better suited with things that can be handled without too much care than with finely detailed scale models with fragile parts that would be better in a display cabinet.

To keep the furniture in proportion, settle on an approximate scale. One-twelfth is commonly used — 1 inch on a model represents 1 foot on the full-size article. This means you are planning for dolls between 5-inches and 6-inches tall in rooms that are 8-inches or 9-inches high. At that scale, a table will be 2½- to 3-inches high, and a chair seat will be about half that. At this scale you can make recognizable furniture, but you cannot include a lot of detail. For instance, you cannot include drawers, but you would have to indicate them by painted and inked outlines. You might put cloth on a seat to indicate upholstery, but you cannot do much about rails in the back.

There are fashion dolls available, which the young owners can dress in many ways; these are about one-fifth or one-sixth scale. They are too big for most doll houses — rooms would have to be 16- to 19-inches high — but a girl may welcome furniture to use with these larger dolls. A table would be 6-inches or more high; with chairs, beds and other furniture at that scale, you can provide more detail without the item being too weak for handling.

You cannot make many things in the same way as their fullsize counterparts. For example, scaled legs and rails would be too fine in section. Many parts will have to be considerably oversized proportionately, although some pieces will have correct overall sizes. Many parts are best cut from solid wood, built up from several pieces in the fullsize object represented by shaped cuts in a single piece of wood.

Plywood offers strength in thin sheets, but watch proportion. If you can get ⅛-inch (3mm) plywood that could form a table top, but at one-twelfth its scale thickness is 1½ inches. Although that is oversize, it is usually acceptable. There are thinner plywoods, but they are difficult to find. Veneers 1/16 inch or less have possibilities, but they have to be backed by framing for durability. Formica and other reinforced plastics are thin enough and strong enough to be used to represent wood up to ¾-inch thick. Of course, any patterns will be out of proportion and would have to be painted over. You may fashion some parts with sheet metal, which can be fastened to wood with epoxy adhesives.

The designs which follow are for use in a one-twelfth scale doll house, unless stated otherwise. They are ideas for basic furniture. You can do much to add realism by painting and detailed line work with a pen. Nearly all parts should be joined with glue only, so use a good glue and clamp joints. In most cases, you cannot use ordinary clamps. You may be able to put on weights, or you can tie with rubber bands. Also, you can wrap with masking tape or other adhesive tape. Allow glue to set thoroughly before doing further work.

A simple chair is cut in one piece from a 1½-inch square section wood (FIG. 4-7A). You can make four or more as quickly as one chair. Mark out a side (FIG. 4-8A) and front on adjoining faces; then, first cut the space between the legs, as viewed from the front (FIG. 4-8B). Turn the chair on its side and cut the curved back (FIG. 4-8C) and then the other cuts. The chair could be finished and used as it is. However, it will look better if you provide a veneer or plastic seat, glued on and overhanging no more than ¹⁄₁₆ inch, with rounded front corners.

A matching table (FIG. 4-7B) is too big to cut across a solid block with a scroll saw. Instead, four identical corners are cut from 1½-inch square wood (FIG. 4-8D and E), then glued together under a plywood or plastic top (FIG. 4-8F). Let the top overhang up to ⅛ inch and round the corners.

A bed or couch can be made to the same scale in a very similar way. Use wood ⁵⁄₁₆-inch thick for the main parts, and ⅛-inch plywood for the additional parts.

A bed length should be 7 inches, but the width may be what you wish—5 inches is suggested (FIG. 4-9A). Cut two side pieces with the grain upwards (FIG. 4-9B), to give strength in the legs. Glue these pieces to the central plain piece (FIG. 4-9C), which will take care of any weakness in the short grain of the sides.

For a divan or low couch, leave the bed at that stage, but you can add a plywood head (FIG. 4-9D) with the shaping of your choice. You could also fit a matching foot, particularly if the doll house is being furnished in a Victorian or oldtime manner.

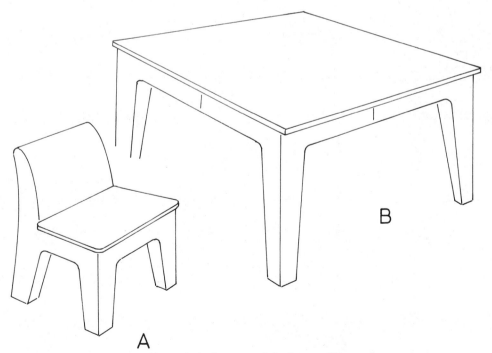

Fig. 4-7. A doll house table and chair cut mainly from solid wood.

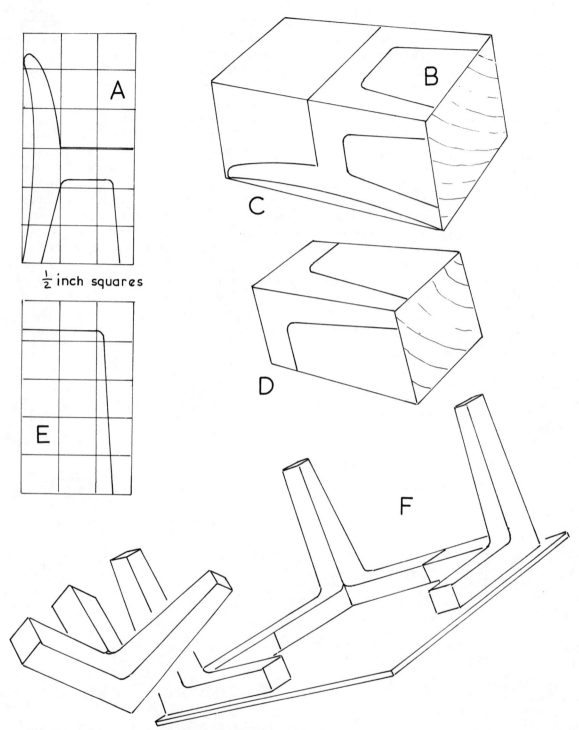

A

½ inch squares

E

B

C

D

F

Fig. 4-8. How to cut the chair and table from solid wood.

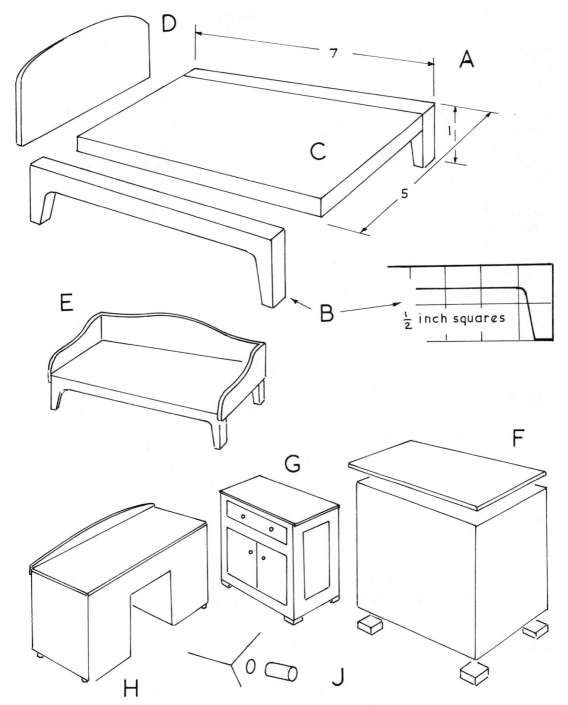

Labels within figure: D, A, C, 7, 1, 5, B, ½ inch squares, E, G, F, H, J

Fig. 4-9. *More doll house furniture to match the chair and table.*

A couch or sofa may have a similar construction (FIG. 4-9E). A suitable size might be 1½-inch seat height and a top 2 inches ×5 inches, but arrange sizes to suit available space. Make the main assembly in the same way as the bed; then, add ⅛-inch plywood shapes, on three sides, just at the back or at the back and one end.

In both cases you might cover most of the wood with fabric to give it a realistic appearance, with pillows and sheets where appropriate. Any wood left exposed should be stained and given a clear finish.

At one-twelfth scale you cannot provide much detail on such things as cupboards, chests, sideboards and stools. They have to be represented by plain blocks of wood; then, details are indicated by painted and ink lining.

A plain block may have feet and could be given a thin slightly overhanging top (FIG. 4-9F). The rest of the scale appearance results from painting (FIG. 4-9G). A desk or dresser could have the block cut away (FIG. 4-9H). Feet can be small squares glued on, or use pieces of ¼-inch dowel rod in holes (FIG. 4-9J). A stool can be made with a solid wood top and dowel rod legs, but watch proportions—a footstool should only be about ¾-inch high.

If you want to make furniture for larger dolls, a scale of one-fifth or one-sixth sizes allows you to use a more realistic construction. Moreover, there is more scope for using the strength of plywood, as ⅛ inch now represents about ¾ inch, and chair seats will be about 3-inches high.

A chair may be framed in ⅛-inch plywood, without parts looking out of proportion (FIG. 4-10A).

Cut two matching plywood sides (FIG. 4-10B). Cut a front with matching leg arrangements (FIG. 4-10C). This will fit between the sides (FIG. 4-10D).

Make a solid wood block ⅜-inch thick (FIG. 4-10E and F). Its front edge should be the same width as the front plywood part (FIG. 4-10G).

Glue the plywood parts to each other and to the seat block. If you think it is necessary, drive a few very fine pins to reinforce the joints.

The seat may be ⅛-inch plywood (FIG. 4-10H and J). If you let it overhang slightly and cover it with cloth wrapped over the rounded edges, it will have an upholstered appearance. Glue it in place.

Make the back (FIG. 4-10K) to overlap with rounded edges, and cover it with cloth to match the seat. Glue and pin it in place.

A fairly dark stain should disguise the exposed plywood edges. Follow this with a clear finish. If you make a set of four chairs, it will be best to do all of each stage to each chair at the same time so they match. Finishing may be completed before the upholstered parts are attached.

Make a table to match the chairs, using plywood and solid wood of the same sections (FIG. 4-11A). If you bevel the edges of the top underneath a little and round them, the top will look lighter. The suggested height is proportional to the chair, but you can alter other sizes to suit available space.

Another method of all-plywood construction could be used for a dining table, but sizes are suggested for a coffee table at one-sixth scale. Use ⅛-inch or 3/16-inch

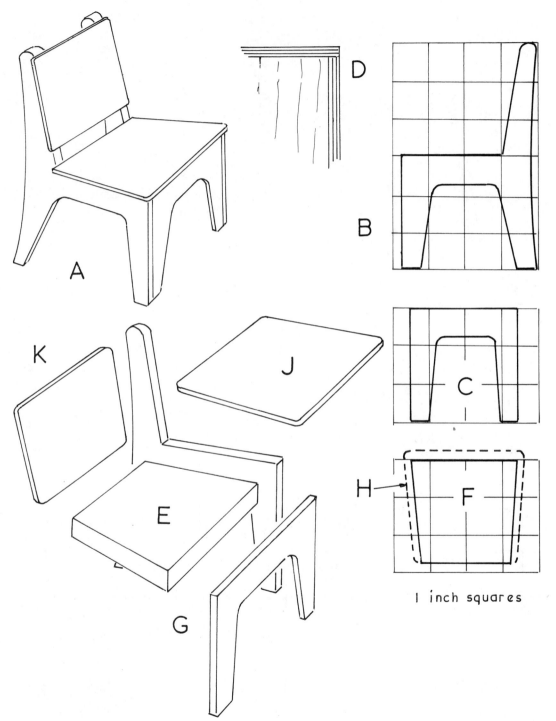

Fig. 4-10. Construction of a framed doll chair.

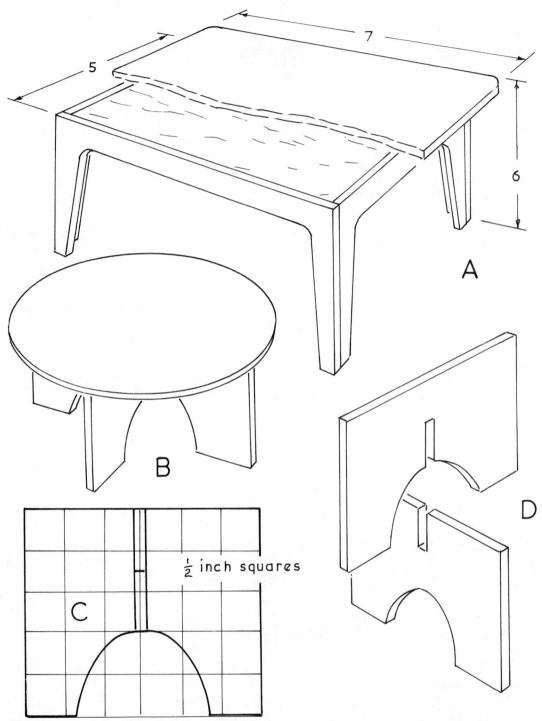

5

7

6

A

B

½ inch squares

C

D

Fig. 4-11. Construction of framed doll tables.

plywood for the legs and ⅛-inch plywood for the top (FIG. 4-11B). The table is drawn with a 3½-inch diameter top standing 2½ inches above the floor.

Make the two legs the same (FIG. 4-11C), except for the mating notches (FIG. 4-11D). Cut the notches to make a tight press fit. A circular top, drawn with a compass, is suggested. Make it octagonal or any other outline. Round its edges.

Glue the legs to each other and check that they are square across. Level the top edges, if necessary; then, invert the leg assembly on the underside of the top. Put a weight on top while the glue sets.

FOLDING FARM

A child playing with cutout animals, small wheeled toys and related equipment will enjoy having an enclosed area in which to move these rather small items. Sectional fences (FIG. 2-6) allow him to arrange his own boundaries, but they may soon be scattered all over the floor with the rest of the toys.

This farm (FIG. 4-12) forms a boxlike assembly that will serve as a ranch, farmyard, zoo or fort, according to the child's needs and imagination. The walls lift off the base and will fold flat for storage, so the farm takes up little room when not in use.

All parts may be ½-inch plywood. The suggested design (FIG. 4-13) assembles to 18-inches square and 6-inches high. The short ends are hinged outside where they meet and inside where they join the longer pieces, so they will fold inwards (FIG. 4-13A). The base (FIG. 4-13B) fits inside the walls and locks to them with projecting lugs (FIG. 4-13C). You could make the farm a different size, but the

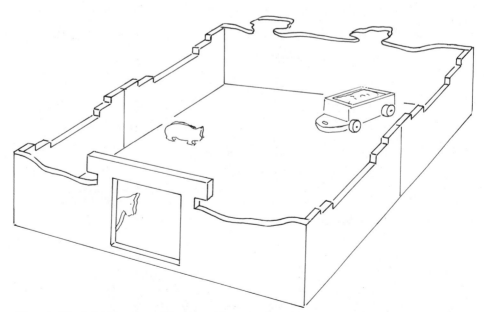

Fig. 4-12. A folding farm for use with animal cutouts.

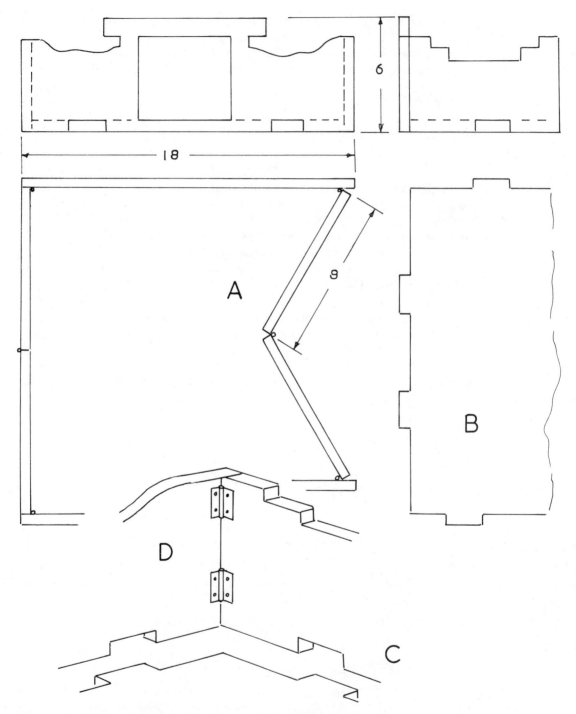

Fig. 4-13. Sizes and construction of parts of the folding farm.

folding parts must be arranged short enough to not meet when folded inside the other parts.

You can arrange any top outline you wish. This example has an entrance in one long side and the opposite side is shaped as if it is a natural hedge with two trees projecting. The short sides are drawn as if in stone, which might also be appropriate for a fort. Whatever outlines you cut, it is helpful to have the hinged parts all the same height and deep enough to provide strength.

Make the front (FIG. 4-14A). Cut the bottom of the entrance the same height as the thickness of the base. Do not cut the top crossbar too shallow, because it has to provide strength when the folded farm is handled. Mark the sockets on the lower edge, but do not cut them until you can match them with the lugs on the base.

The back (FIG. 4-14B) has the same length and corner heights, but you can shape the top in any way you wish. The sockets are at a different spacing from the front.

The four side sections (FIG. 4-14C) are the same, although you could vary the top patterns, provided that you kept the meeting ends at the same height.

Use the surrounding parts as a guide to the size of the base (FIG. 4-14D). When the other parts are assembled, they should press down on it so it fits inside tightly and the sockets grip the lugs.

Check each edge against the part it has to join. Sockets and lug spacings are different back and front, so there should be no difficulty trying to fit a symmetrical base, which might not be quite accurate.

The best hinges are cut from long lengths of piano hinge, but two 1-inch or 1½-inch hinges at each position should be satisfactory (FIG. 4-13D).

You can choose between a simple finish with one color all over, or a more detailed paint treatment. The base could be a light brown or green. Wood around the entrance may be a dark brown. Stones can be a deeper brown and any foliage a darker green. You could line in details, such as joints in the stonework or a base for a hedge.

Materials List for Folding Farm

(all ½-inch plywood)	
1 front	6 × 19
1 back	6 × 19
4 sides	6 × 9
1 base	18 × 18

RING GAME

Throwing rings onto hooks makes a good competitive game. This hanging board and rings (FIG. 4-15) will appeal to younger users, but others may want to join in. Getting a ring on a hook should be fairly easy when standing a short distance away, but older users can make it more difficult at a greater distance.

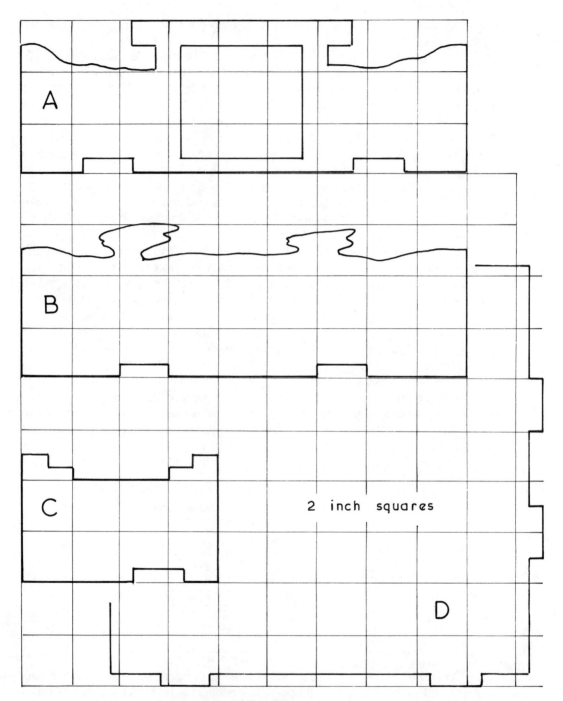

Fig. 4-14. *The shapes of parts of the folding farm.*

2 inch squares

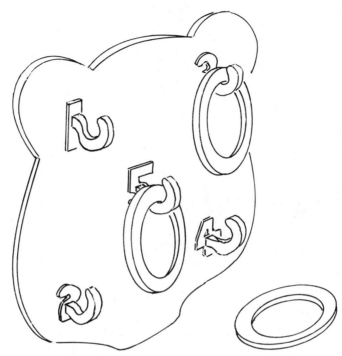

Fig. 4-15. All parts of this ring board are made with a scroll saw.

All parts are plywood. The rings will be stronger if cut from plywood made from five veneers instead of the more common three. The hooks could also be cut from solid wood, with the grain from front to back.

These drawings are for a game with a board about 14-inches each way. You could alter sizes larger or smaller by using grids of different size squares. The suggested sizes should suit young children, without the parts being clumsy.

Start by marking out the five hooks (Fig. 4-16A), ½-inch thick. Cut square tenons to go through a figure and the back board. Round the projecting parts of each hook. Finish all five to a uniform appearance.

The figures (Fig. 4-16B and 17) are ¼-inch thick. Draw them around ½-inch square holes to take the hooks. Make sure enough wood is left around the holes, but the back board will provide strength when the parts are assembled. Round the front edges.

The square holes on the back board locate the figures and hooks (Fig. 4-18). Draw and cut the outline; then round its front edges.

Check the fit of the hooks through the figures and the back board. If you intend painting one color all over, glue the parts together now, but if you will be using different colors, you may prefer to paint parts before the assembly. Having the figures in a contrasting color to the other parts emphasizes them and highlights the hooks.

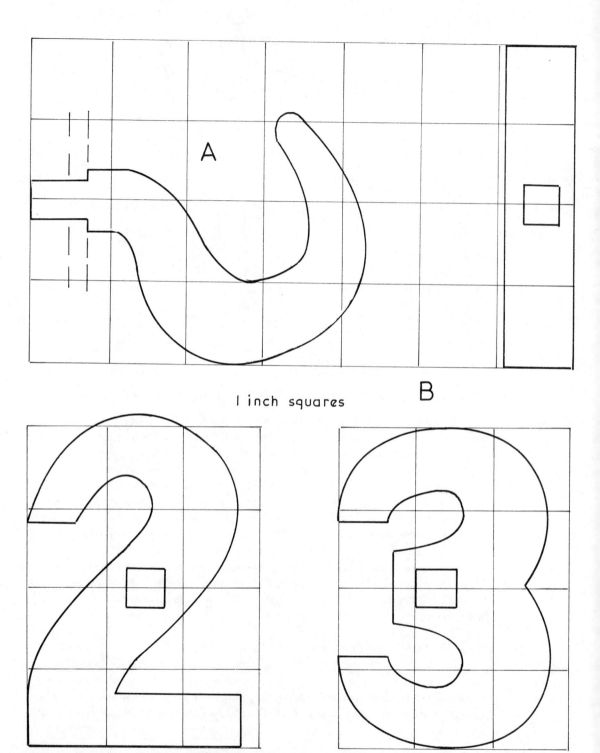

A

1 inch squares

B

Fig. 4-16. Details of parts of the ring board.

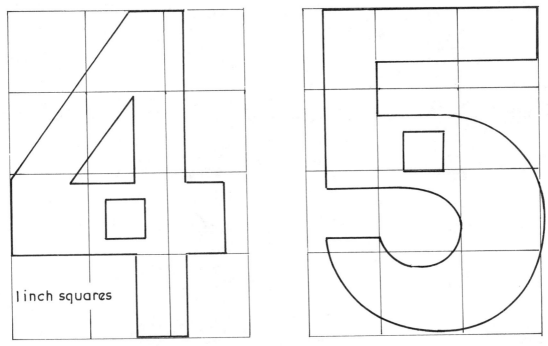

1 inch squares

Fig. 4-17. More figures for the ring board.

You may wish to experiment with the sizes of rings to test the ease of throwing onto hooks, but a 4-inch round hole with a ¾-inch border may be satisfactory. With strong plywood, you could reduce the width of the border. Make at least three rings. Round their edges.

The board could be screwed to a wall, or you could put a large screw eye in the top edge to hang on a hook or nail.

Materials List for Ring Game

5 hooks	3½ × 5 × ½
Figures from	3 × 19 × ¼
1 back board	14 × 15 × ½

VICTORIAN STICK TOYS

In the last century, children enjoyed playing with toys where the movement of two sticks over each other caused figures to perform actions. These were made of wood in large variety. Even today, a young child will get a lot of fun out of performing a simple action and getting results. Two of these toys are described here: two workers on an anvil and an acrobat.

Use compact hardwood, as some parts have to be strong when cross-grained. The toys are described in basic form. You could do some shaping of bodies and

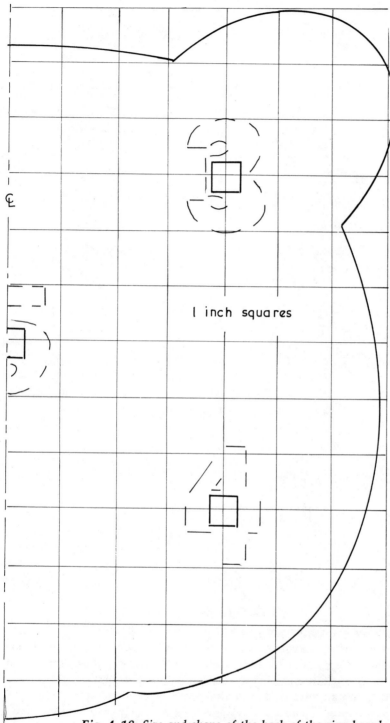

1 inch squares

Fig. 4-18. *Size and shape of the back of the ring board.*

add painted clothing and other features, but a child will probably get as much enjoyment out of the action of the basic figures as when you have spent much time decorating them to adult-satisfying standards.

Anvil Workers

This toy consists of two identical men with hammers astride two long sticks. As the sticks are moved backwards and forwards, the men take turns hitting an anvil between them (FIG. 4-19A).

Prepare two sticks $3/8$-inch $\times 1/2$-inch section at least 18-inches long. Consider cutting the sticks too long; then, trim them after the young user has tried the action.

Mark out the men (FIG. 4-19B) on wood 1-inch thick. Cut the outlines. Drill $1/8$-inch holes through the legs, as marked, $9/16$-inch apart.

Cut the legs to fit over the $3/8$-inch way of the sticks (FIG. 4-19C). Trim the opening to clear the top stick as the men move (FIG. 4-19D). Clearance in individual toys may vary, so you might have to adjust this after a trial assembly.

Make each mallet head with a $3/4$-inch length of $3/8$-inch dowel rod, or it could be a square section. The handle is $1/8$-inch diameter wire (FIG. 4-19E).

Reduce the thickness of the arm (FIG. 4-19F). Join these parts with epoxy glue.

Overlap the sticks about 13 inches. Mark the center of the overlap and position the men $4^{1}/2$-inches each side of this center. Drill $1/8$-inch holes at these positions in the top sticks, and fit the men over with nails or cotter pins through temporarily. Tilt one man so his hammer is down, and mark and drill through the bottom stick. Put a pin through, and tilt the assembly so the other man lowers his hammer. Put an awl through the lower hole in the leg, and try the action. If one man hits while the other lifts, with the action both ways, drill the lower stick there.

Put a piece of $1/8$-inch wood as an anvil at the center of the top piece (FIG. 4-19G). Metal might make a more satisfying noise.

Paint the men and the anvil, but it will probably be better to leave the sticks untreated.

Assemble with cotter pins (FIG. 4-19H). Use long soft metal rivets. Nails could be taken through undersize holes and filed level.

Acrobat

This toy (FIG. 4-20) also has two sticks sliding over each other, so they work a figure which has arms and legs pivoted to the body. Sliding one stick along the other makes the acrobat perform tricks on the top of the long stick. As with the other toy, you can leave the parts of the figure plain, or you can do some shaping and add detail with paint.

Prepare the two sticks. Although both are nominally $1/2$-inch square, the long one should be planed slightly thinner than the other, so the handle will slide easily on it.

Cut the body (FIG. 4-20A and B). It should be the same thickness as the thicker stick.

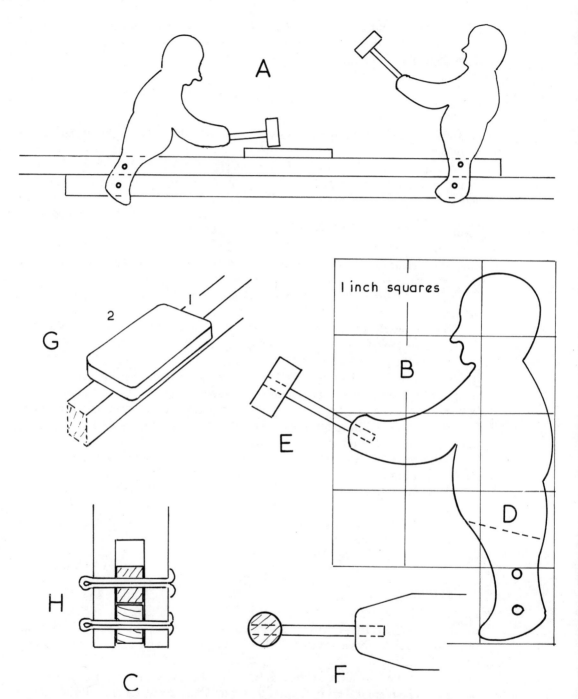

Fig. 4-19. *Moving the sticks backwards and forwards make the men hit the anvil.*

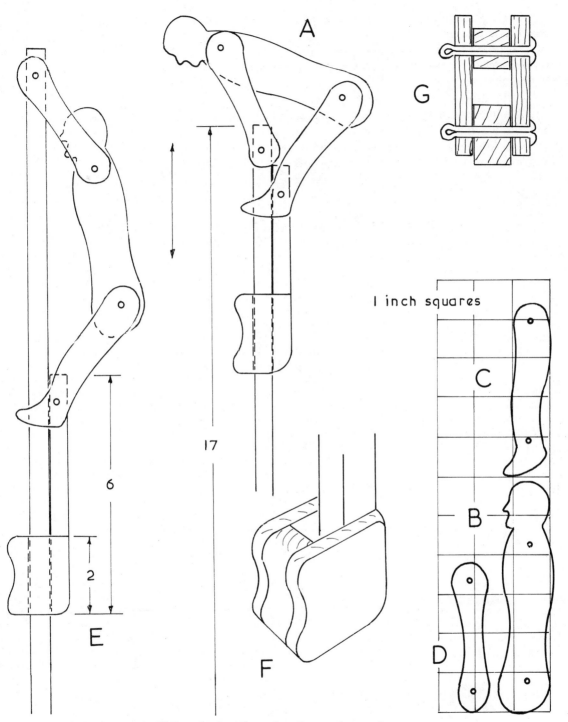

A

G

1 inch squares

C

B

D

17

6

2

E

F

Fig. 4-20. Sliding the handle makes the acrobat perform.

Cut the pair of legs (FIG. 4-20C) and the pair of arms (FIG. 4-20D) from thinner wood. Round the outer edges of these pieces.

Make the handle (FIG. 4-20E and F) with a spacer the same thickness as the shorter stick and cheeks ¼-inch thick. The long stick should slide easily in the gap. Round all outer edges.

Drill all body parts and the sticks, where indicated, for ⅛-inch cotter pins.

Remove any sharp edges or corners. Paint the figure parts. It will probably be better to leave the sticks untreated.

Join the legs and arms to the body with cotter pins, with enough clearance to allow movement. Join the arms and legs to the sticks in a similar way (FIG. 4-20G). Try the action before finally closing these cotter pins, in case any adjustment is needed.

Materials List for Victorian Stick Toys

Anvil Workers	
2 sticks	⅜ × ½ × 18
2 figures	1 × 3 × 5
1 anvil	¼ × 1 × 3
Acrobat	
1 stick	½ × ½ × 18
1 stick	½ × ½ × 7
1 body	½ × ½ × 7
2 arms	¼ × 1 × 5
2 legs	¼ × 1 × 6

Five

Large Toys

Besides toys which may be handled and used by all ages of children and which may usually be stored in a box after use, there are others which are big enough to be regarded as child-size furniture. Others can be sat on or in, and may be hidden. Except for those which have to be made of very thick wood, most of these toys can have the bulk of the work done on a scroll saw.

Plywood can be used for parts of many larger toys; this has the advantage of strength without excessive thickness. Also, it is easy to cut on your saw. Some other parts may be softwood, provided that you avoid resinous or splintery wood and round all edges that might be troublesome for young hands.

Sizes of parts for the projects in this chapter should be within the range of most scroll saws; although, you might have to turn the blades across for some longer cuts. Plan ahead, and do related cuts at the same time; although, it might not be possible to cut two thicknesses at the same time. Where parts have to mate with each other or joints cut, check the pieces against each other for sizes, and do not just depend on shapes shown on drawings. Wood may vary, or you may cut one side of a vital line on one piece and the opposite side on the other. Precision might not be so important in some toys, but accuracy should appeal to your ideas of craftsmanship.

GERMAN CRADLE

A young girl will welcome a cradle or crib for her doll, but it is very easy to make what amounts to little more than a box. This cradle (FIG. 5-1) is based on German originals, with a hood over the head and rockers which can be kept moving with a foot while sitting alongside. Sizes suggested will suit a doll up to

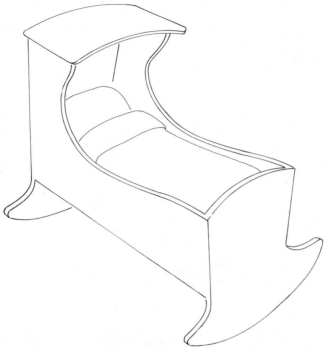

Fig. 5-1. This doll cradle is based on a German original.

14-inches tall. Overall sizes are then 16-inches long, 14-inches wide and 15-inches high (FIG. 5-2A).

All parts are plywood, with most of it ½-inch thick. Hardwood plywood would be attractive with a clear finish, but softwood plywood would be lighter and could be given a painted finish, possibly with decals. Corners are joined with finger joints (FIG. 5-4A), which can be cut completely with a scroll saw. With pins driven each way, they cannot be pulled apart without breaking.

The main parts link together with finger joints; then, the bottom fits inside and the curved hood is supported by the back and an arched piece (FIG. 5-2B).

Mark out the back about a centerline (FIG. 5-3A). Do not draw the bottom curve with a compass. It is flattened towards the center so the cradle will settle level when left alone. Cut the outline, including the joints.

Mark out the front so it matches, but is stopped at the lower curved top edge (FIG. 5-3B). Cut it to shape. In both cases the ends of the fingers should be left a little too long, so they can be planed level after assembly.

Mark out the pair of sides (FIG. 5-4B). Compare the joints with the parts they have to meet. Allow for any variations. Number the meeting corners, so they will fit together in the intended way. Leave a little extra wood on the ends of the fingers. Bevel the top edges to match the curve of the hood (FIG. 5-4C).

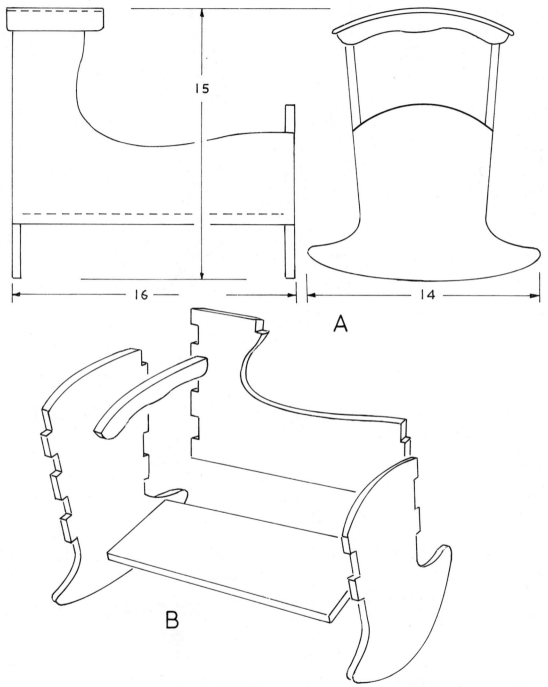

A

B

Fig. 5-2. Sizes and assembly of the doll cradle.

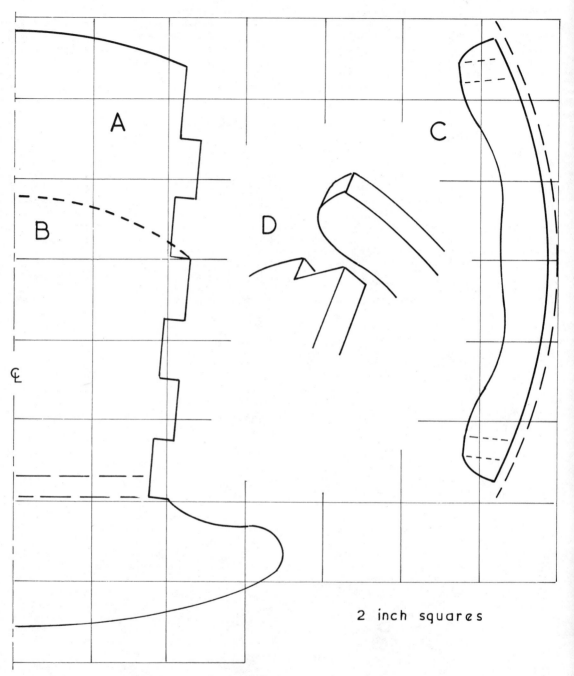

A

B

C

D

℄

2 inch squares

Fig. 5-3. Sizes of crosswise parts of the doll cradle.

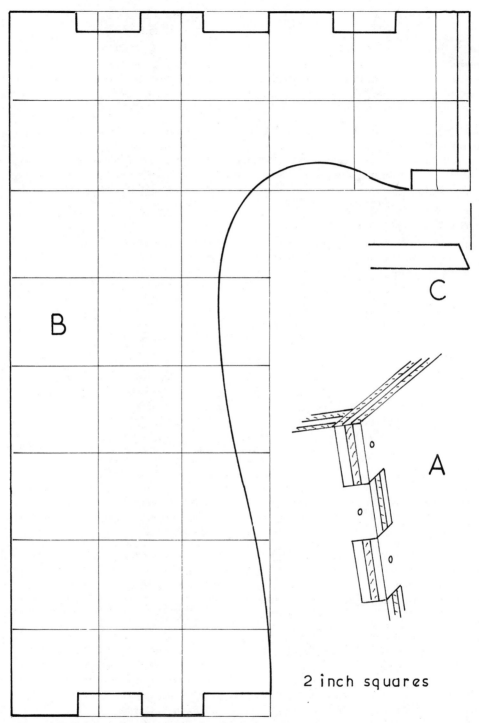

B

C

A

2 inch squares

Fig. 5-4. Sides and corner joints for the doll cradle.

Round and sand all the edges that will be exposed in the assembled cradle.

Join the parts made so far. Use glue and a fine pin centrally in each finger. Set it below the surface, and cover its head with wood filler. Level any projecting ends of fingers.

Make the bottom to fit inside the other parts. Bevel to suit the sides. Position it at or close to the bottom edges of the sides. Secure it with glue and a few pins.

Make the arch (FIG. 5-3C) with a curve to match that of the back; it extends through the notches in the sides (FIG. 5-3D). Round the lower edge and the extending ends.

Join the arch piece to the sides with glue and pins. Do any leveling necessary to allow a smooth curve for the hood top.

Make the top from thin plywood. It will blend easiest if the grain of the outside veneers is in the direction of the length of the cradle. Cut it to overhang ½-inch all around. Round the edges and corners.

Attach it with glue and pins. Start at one side and work across. If there is much resistance to bending, use a few fine screws into the sides. Clamp by tying cords over the hood and under the cradle.

A painted finish may be the same way all over, or you could use a lighter color inside. Appropriate decals might be used on the ends.

Materials List for German Cradle

(all plywood)	
1 back	½ × 14 × 16
1 front	½ × 14 × 12
2 sides	½ × 12 × 17
1 bottom	½ × 8 × 16
1 top	⅛ × 6 × 10

ROCKING HORSE

A fully shaped and lifelike rocking horse involves thicker wood than could be cut on a scroll saw, but this rocking horse (FIG. 5-5) will look what it is meant to be in the eyes of its user. This is a small rocking horse intended for a young child. It is 29-inches long over the rockers, stands 21-inches high and is 12-inches across the base. Paint on features and details of reins and possibly add fur to represent a mane, but the toy is shown plain.

All wood is ¾-inch thick, so it is easily cut, whether you use hardwood or softwood. Parts are glued and nailed or screwed together.

The body is built up with the head and tail pieces at the center; then, body pieces go each side and the legs go outside again, to make up a total thickness of 3½ inches, which is covered by the seat (FIG. 5-6A and B). The legs extend to two platforms which go across the two rockers (FIG. 5-6C). Parts are best made from the center outwards, so you can check some sizes against each other.

Mark out and cut the head (FIG. 5-7A). For the strongest construction position the grain direction from the ear to the rear bottom corner. Leave the edges that will

Fig. 5-5. All parts of this rocking horse are made with a scroll saw.

be covered by other parts square, but well round all exposed edges. Drill for a
⅝-inch dowel handle (FIG. 5-7B). Round its ends and glue it in.

Make the tail section (FIG. 5-7C). Arrange the grain in the direction of the
length of the tail. Most of this part will come between the body sides and should
be left square, but round the extending tail.

The body sides are straight (FIG. 5-8A), and the ends curved. At the rear, the
curve should match that of the tail section. At the front, the head section is
forward of the body (FIG. 5-6D). Round the outer edges of the curved ends. Leave
the top edges square. Most of the body sides will be covered by the legs, and any
edges left exposed after fitting the legs may be rounded later.

Join the body parts to the head and tail sections, using glue and a few nails or
screws. Many screw or nail heads can be arranged to be covered by legs.

Cut two pairs of legs (FIG. 5-9A and B). Leave rounding any edges until you
have tried them in position and marked the location on the body sides.

Try two legs in position on the body, using FIG. 5-6 as a guide. The distance
between the hooves should be 11 inches. Top edges of the legs should come level
with the flat top edge of the body. Mark where the legs should be on the body
sides and mark on the legs how much they project below the body.

Well round the projecting parts of the legs. Round what will be the outer
edges of the parts of legs overlapping the body.

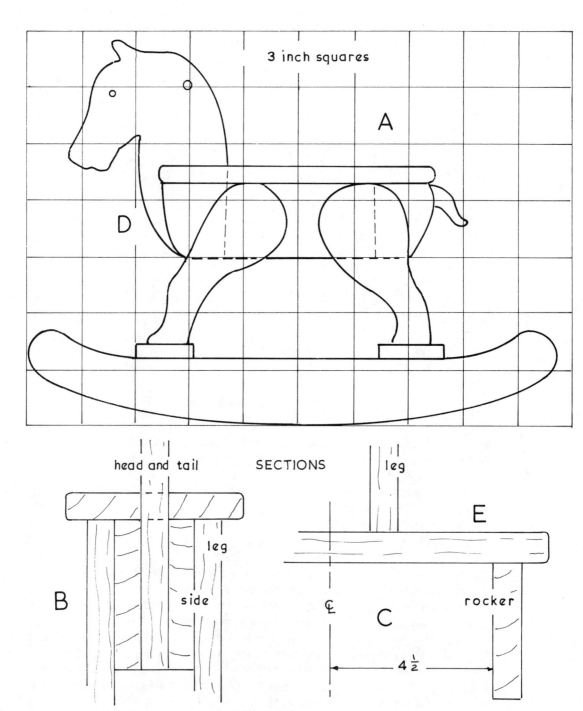

3 inch squares

A

D

head and tail   SECTIONS   leg

B   side   leg   E   rocker

C   4½

Fig. 5-6. Sizes and sections of the rocking horse.

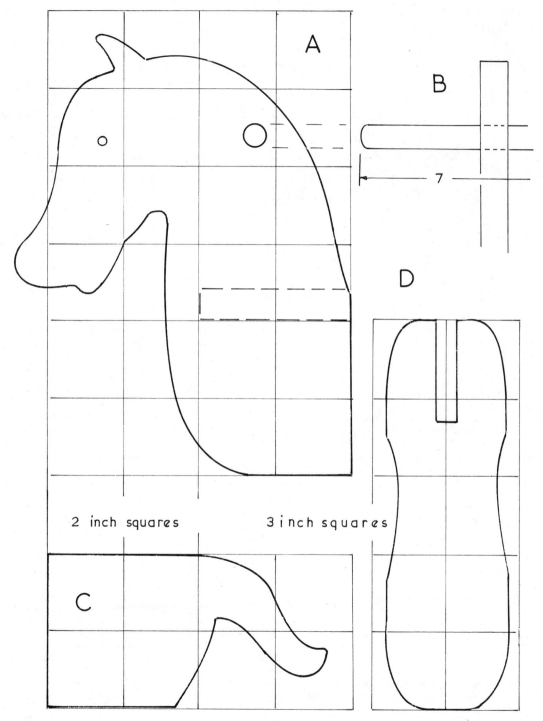

2 inch squares   3 inch squares

Fig. 5-7. Parts of the horse and seat.

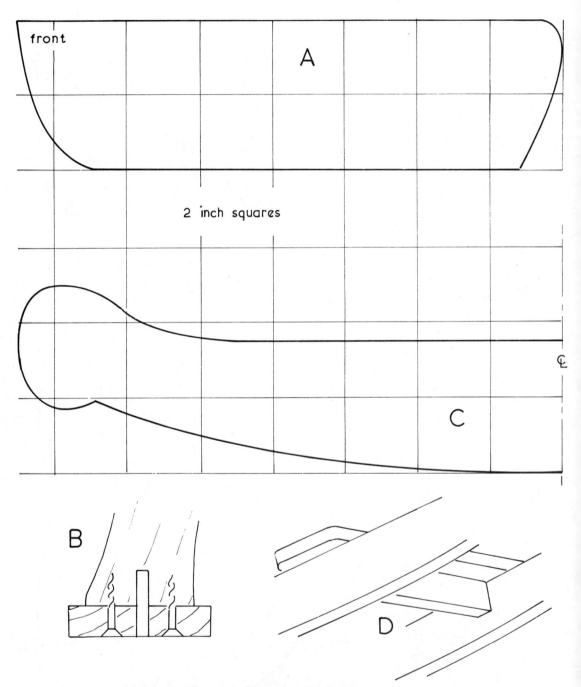

front

A

2 inch squares

C

B

D

Fig. 5-8. Parts of the horse and rockers. Some assembly details.

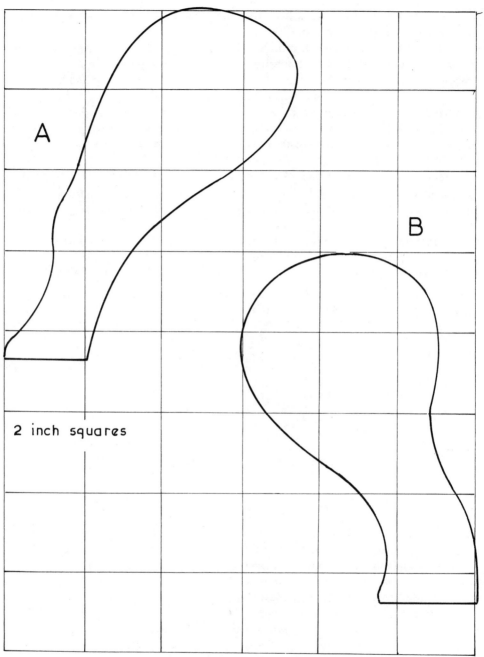

A

B

2 inch squares

Fig. 5-9. Legs for the rocking horse.

Join the legs to the body. Check that the assembled horse stands upright. If not, take a little off one or more hoofs.

Make the seat to match the other parts (FIG. 5-7D). The slot fits around the head. Well round all edges. Attach the seat to the other parts. When the toy is finished, add some padding to the seat for comfort and a simulated saddle.

The platforms (FIG. 5-6E) are parallel strips 12-inches long and extending 3/4-inch over the rockers. Round the corners and edges that will project.

Fix the platforms to the ends of the legs. You could use long screws only, but the strongest joints would be with a central 1/4-inch dowel and two screws (FIG. 5-8B) in each joint.

Make two matching rockers (FIG. 5-8C). They have smooth bottom curves with projections at each end to resist a user tilting the horse too far. The central flat top section takes the platforms. Round bottom edges to minimize damage to floor coverings.

It may be strong enough to screw the platforms to the rockers, but you can improve stiffness by putting strips across under the platforms (FIG. 5-8D).

Check over for any roughness or excess glue; then finish with paint.

Materials List for Rocking Horse

1 head	$3/4 \times$	7×14
1 handle	$8 \times 5/8$ diameter	
1 tail	$3/4 \times$	6×9
2 bodies	$3/4 \times$	4×16
1 seat	$3/4 \times$	7×16
2 front legs	$3/4 \times$	5×12
2 rear legs	$3/4 \times 5\frac{1}{2} \times 11$	
2 platforms	$3/4 \times$	4×14
2 rockers	$3/4 \times$	5×32
2 stiffeners	$3/4$	2×11

WHEELBARROW

A toddler may have difficulty in managing a wheelbarrow with a single wheel. This barrow (FIG. 5-10) has two wheels, and the handles are spaced to suit a child up to age four. It is capable of carrying all that he can manage and tip, as well as being suitable for transporting toys or giving dolls a ride.

The main parts are 1/2-inch plywood with stiffening provided by softwood strips. Wheels are 5 inches in diameter.

The side view is like a conventional wheelbarrow (FIG. 5-11A), but the sides are not flared, to simplify construction. Obtain the wheels first. It is assumed they will be 5 inches in diameter and about 1-inch thick, able to fit on a steel rod axle 3/8 inch in diameter. Alter sizes a little if yours are very different.

The pair of plywood sides (FIG. 5-12A) set the sizes for many other parts. Mark and cut them first.

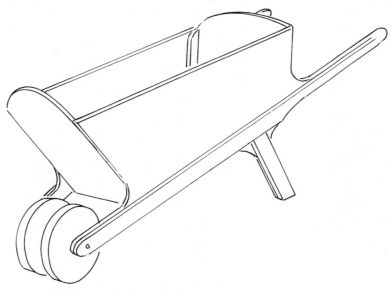

Fig. 5-10. A double-wheeled small wheelbarrow.

Make the stiffening strips which extend from the wheel end and form the handles (Fig. 5-11B). Reduce the handle ends to 1 inch to match the plywood. Attach these strips with glue and nails or screws from inside (Fig. 5-11C).

The handle ends are now 1-inch square, made up of solid wood and plywood. Reduce the section to round far enough to provide a grip; then round the ends. Sand the handles thoroughly.

Stiffen the legs with more strips (Fig. 5-11D). Take the sharpness off the outer edges of all stiffening strips.

At the wheel ends, drill through ⅛-inch holes to mark the axle positions. The holes will be enlarged to suit the axle after assembly.

Make the back (Fig. 5-12B) and front (Fig. 5-12C) pieces. Sides are parallel. Round the section of the top edges.

Put support strips (Fig. 5-11E and 12D) inside the sides to take the bottom, but keep them back far enough from the positions of the ends to allow these in.

Prepare strips to fit inside the four corners (Fig. 5-11F and 12E). Do not fit yet.

Fit the back and front between the sides with glue and a few nails, or use thin screws from the outside. With this assembly as a guide, make the bottom to drop in on the supporting strips.

Glue and screw the bottom in place. Fit the corner strips above the bottom. Screws will pull and hold the parts together better than nails.

Enlarge the holes for the axle, pointing the drill towards the hole in the opposite side, to allow for the taper.

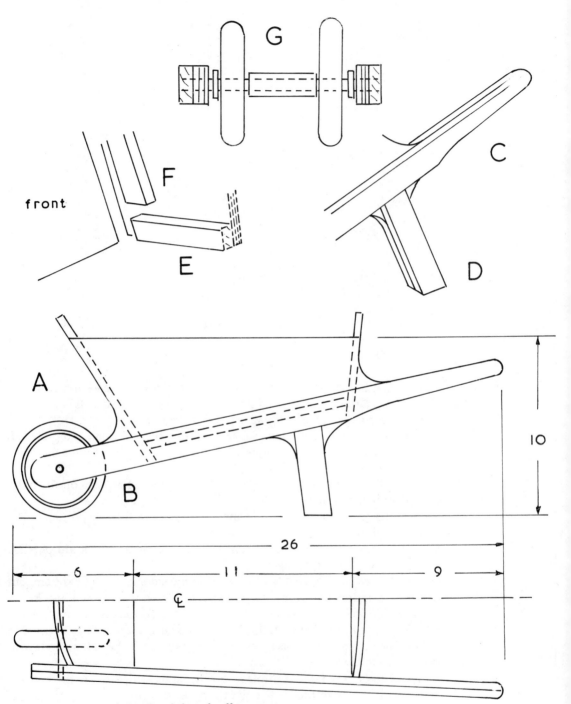

front

Fig. 5-11. *Sizes and details of the wheelbarrow.*

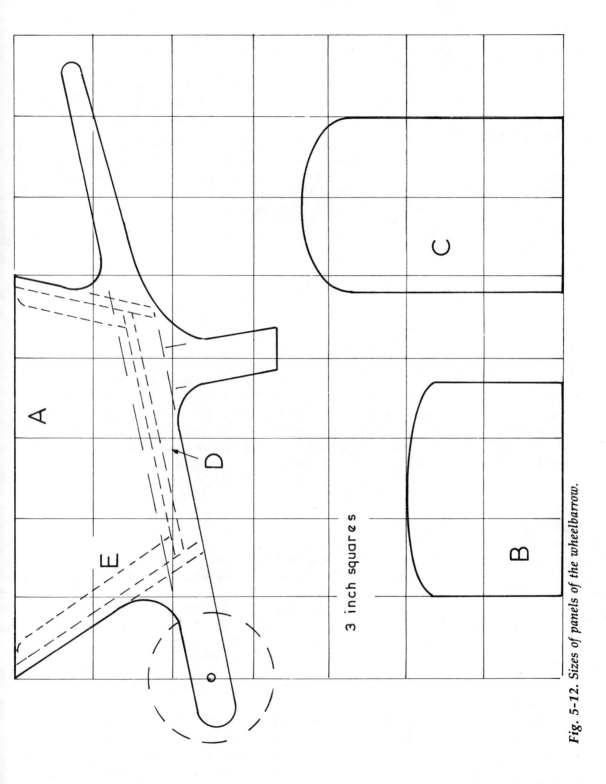

A

D

E

B

C

3 inch squares

Fig. 5-12. Sizes of panels of the wheelbarrow.

The wheels must have some clearance at the sides, which you can arrange with washers. To keep them apart, cut a piece of metal tube to fit over the axle (FIG. 5-11G). The tube need not be a close fit on the axle.

Assemble the wheels and axle. If the axle is a drive fit through the wood, it should not need any other fixing, but you could secure it with epoxy glue.

Round all exposed edges and sand all parts that will be handled. A painted finish is appropriate.

Materials List for Wheelbarrow

2 sides	10 × 26 × ½ plywood
1 back	7 × 9 × ½ plywood
1 front	8 × 11 × ½ plywood
1 bottom	9 × 12 × ½ plywood
2 stiffeners	½ × 1½ × 27
2 legs	½ × 1½ × 7
2 supports	½ × ¾ × 13
2 corner strips	½ × ¾ × 10
2 corner strips	½ × ¾ × 6

SAND BOX AND TOOLS

Digging in sand is always popular with children, but a pile of sand soon becomes an untidy mess. It needs a box to keep it and the children's activities within bounds. This box (FIG. 5-13) will hold a worthwhile amount of sand. The lips around the edges will limit the amount that is spilled over the edges; in addition, the cover keeps off rain and animals. The wavy edges may suggest waves at the seashore to the young users. With this box, you can make a variety of tools, mostly different from those that could be bought.

Top and bottom are ½-inch exterior grade plywood, cut from one standard sheet. Other parts are 1-inch solid wood. You could use dovetails or other interlocking joints, but nails or screws are sufficient. The sizes suggested (FIG. 5-14) allow for the lid to be made from a half sheet of plywood. If you choose other sizes, give the lid a very easy fit over the box.

Make the two sides (FIG. 5-14A) tapered from 11 inches to 5 inches.

Make the back and front to fit between them. Bevel the top edges to match the slope of the sides.

Nail or screw these parts together, and nail on the plywood bottom. You could use waterproof glue in the joints as well.

The rims are 4-inches wide on three sides, but the one on the low edge (FIG. 5-14B) may be 5 inches or wider, as that is where the risk of sand being spread over the edge is greatest.

Cut the pieces to fit on top of the box, and meet at the corners with a support strip underneath (FIG. 5-15A).

Make a template (FIG. 5-15B) to mark the wavy edges uniformly. The waves are 3-inch centers and ½-inch deep. A template twice the length shown would make marking out easier. Cut it from thin plywood or hardboard.

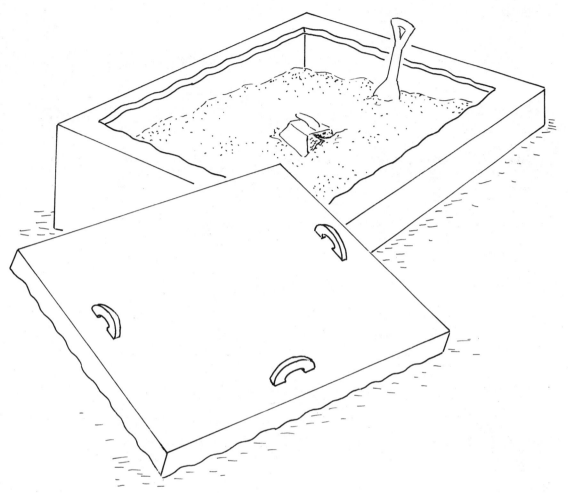

Fig. 5-13. This sand box has a protective lid.

Take sharpness off the edges, and nail or screw the rim pieces to the box. Level outer edges and round edges and corners.

Make the lid (FIG. 5-14C) with a frame of 1-inch × 2-inch strips cut with wavy lower edges (FIG. 5-14D).

Three handles for the lid are shown (FIG. 5-13 and 14E), so the lid can be tilted off using the one handle at the front, or two people can lift from opposite sides.

The handles should be satisfactory made from softwood, but they would be stronger cut from hardwood. Cut to the outline (FIG. 5-15C). Leave the bottom edges flat, but round all other parts, particularly edges that will be gripped. Join the handles to the lid with two screws at each end, driven upwards through the plywood.

The box is best set on stones or concrete, rather than bare earth, which might make the box and contents damp. When full of sand the box will be very heavy, so

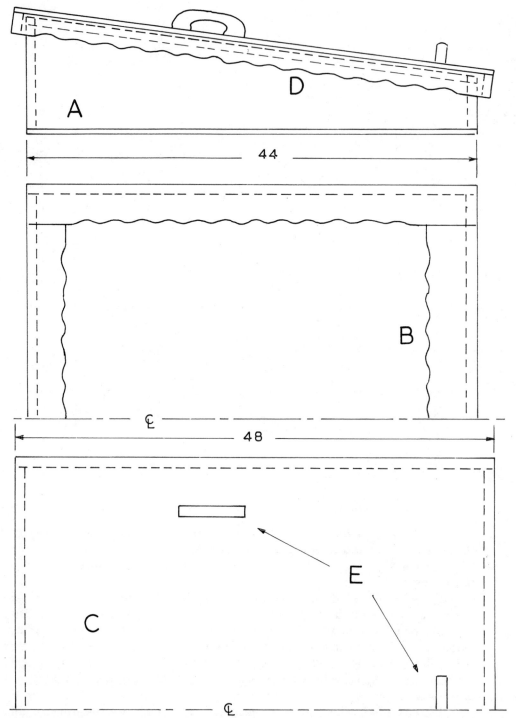

Fig. 5-14. Sizes of the sand box and its lid.

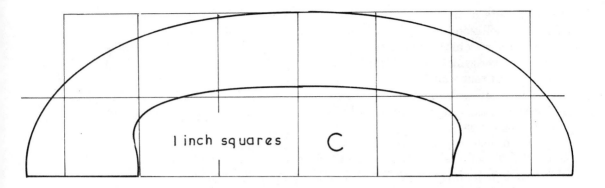

1 inch squares   C

$\frac{3}{4}$ inch squares   B

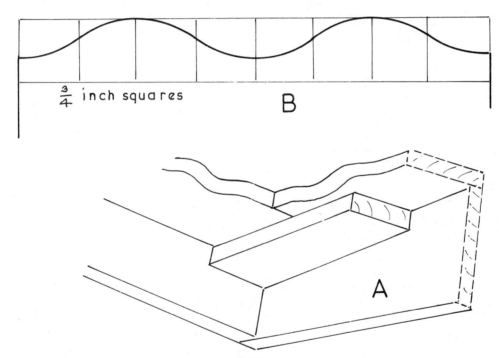

A

Fig. 5-15. Shaped parts of the sand box and details of a corner.

it is best to decide on one position and leave it there. Treating with preservative is advisable. You could leave the wood without further treatment or it might be painted brightly in contrast to the sand.

TOOLS

Buckets are probably best bought as metal or plastic types, but most other tools a child needs to play with in sand can be made with the aid of a scroll saw.

Exterior grade plywood can be used for some tools, but a tough close-grained hardwood will stand up well to the abrasive effects of sand.

A spade may have a loop handle (FIG. 5-16A) or a child may prefer a T handle (FIG. 5-16B). These may be cut from ½-inch wood. Thin the working end to about ³⁄₁₆ inch, and round all the parts that will be handled.

A child can use two scrapers (FIG. 5-16C) to draw together quantities of sand or to level a surface. Cut from plywood ½-inch or less thick. Round the shaped part and the hand hole.

An alternative scraper can be pulled (FIG. 5-16D). Make the blade from plywood (FIG. 5-16E) in a similar way to the other scraper. Cut the handle to an ax shape from ⅝-inch wood (FIG. 5-16F). Join the parts with two screws.

An alternative to a spade is a trowel, which can be used for digging and for smoothing a surface. One can be made with a solid wood or a plywood blade. There are two possible blade outlines (FIG. 5-17A and B). Thin the underside of a ⅜-inch solid wood blade towards the point and edges.

Cut the handle from solid ⅝-inch thick wood (FIG. 5-17C). Round the parts that will be gripped. Join it to the blade with screws from below.

Materials List for Sand Box and Tools

Sand box		
2 sides	1 ×	11 × 46
1 front	1 ×	5 × 45
1 back	1 ×	11 × 45
1 bottom	44 ×	44 × ½ plywood
3 rims	1 ×	4 × 46
1 rim	1 ×	5 × 46
4 lid sides	1 ×	2 × 50
1 top	48 ×	48 × ½ plywood
3 handles	1 ×	2 × 9
Spade		
1 piece	½ ×	3 × 20
Scraper		
1 blade	6 ×	9 × ¼ plywood
1 handle	⅝ × 1½ × 11	
Trowel		
1 blade	⅜ ×	4 × 8
1 handle	¾ ×	2 × 8
Scoop		
2 sides	½ ×	4 × 10
1 back	½ ×	3 × 10
1 top	16 ×	10 × ¼ plywood
1 bottom	10 ×	10 × ¼ plywood
1 handle	¾ ×	2 × 8

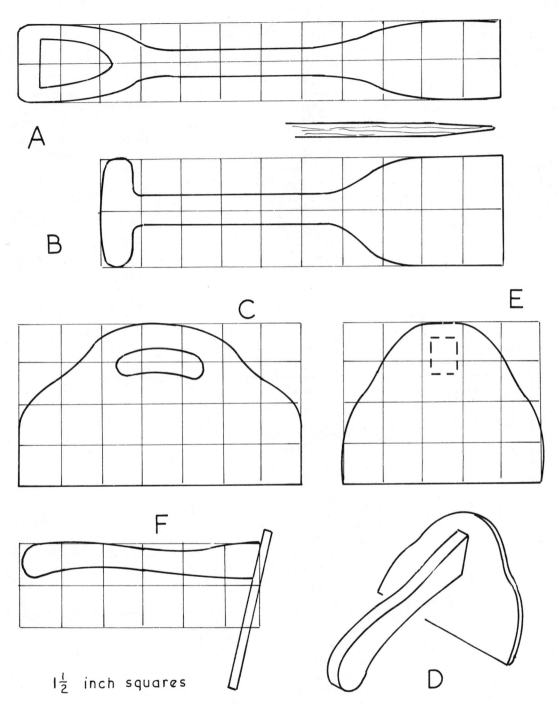

A

B

C

E

F

$1\frac{1}{2}$ inch squares

D

Fig. 5-16. Outlines of tools to use in the sand box.

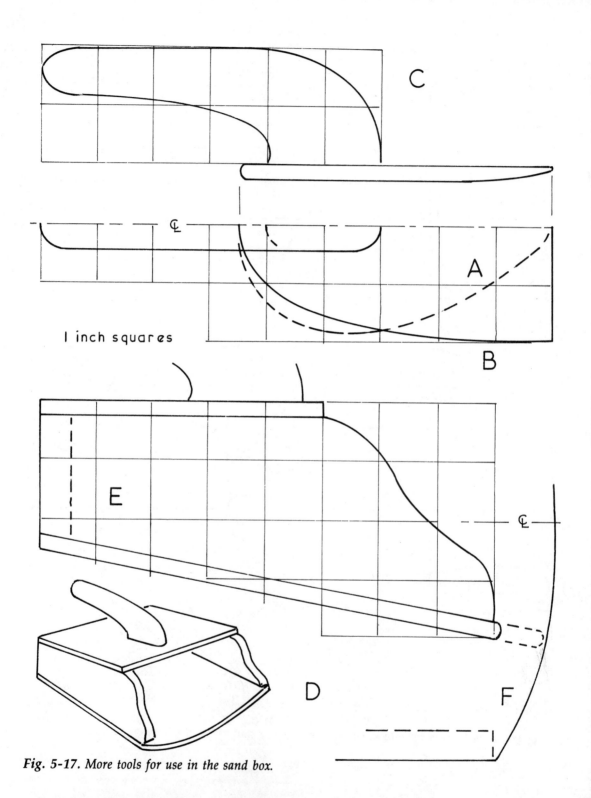

C

A

B

1 inch squares

E

D

F

Fig. 5-17. More tools for use in the sand box.

A scoop (FIG. 5-17D) adds interest to shifting sand. This one has ½-inch solid wood sides and back (FIG. 5-17E). The top is plywood cut straight across. The bottom is plywood with a curved edge (FIG. 5-17F).

Nail the parts together and add a handle, the same as on a trowel.

JUNIOR GO KART

An arrangement of boards on wheels is often improvised by a child, not always successfully or safely. This go kart (FIG. 5-18) will do all a child wants, and more, while his parents will be satisfied that it is as safe as it can be. There is a box seat, and steering is by a rope or by the feet. The front axle assembly can be altered to suit leg lengths, for different children or as the one user grows taller. A tow rope may be fitted through the front hole; in addition, there may be a rear handle for an adult to control and push a small child.

Nearly all the wood is ¾-inch thick. Softwood is suitable, so the many curves are easily cut with a scroll saw. Wheels 6 inches in diameter on ⅜-inch steel axles are suggested, but differences will not matter. You could have the wheels larger at

Fig. 5-18. The junior go kart is adjustable for size and may be steered by feet, or a rope and can be pushed with a handle.

the back than the front. Parts may be glued and nailed or screwed, although you may prefer to use dovetails or finger joints on the corners of the box seat; these are the corners liable to most stress.

Sizes suggested (Fig. 5-19A) should suit children up to at least age five. For a particular child you may wish to measure him before starting work. Allow for growth.

The long central members (Fig. 5-19B) forms the chassis on which the other parts fit. Cut it to shape (Fig. 5-20A). Holes have to suit the pivot bolt for the front axle assembly. Do not drill them until you have the other parts ready.

Make the bottom of the seat (Fig. 5-19C). This might have to be made up from two or more boards, which should be glued; although, joining to other parts will hold them in place. The hollows in the front edge (Fig. 5-20B) should blend into the curves of the central piece. Well round the upper edges of these hollows, for comfort.

The two sides of the seat (Fig. 5-19D and 21A) fit on top of the seat bottom, and the seat back (Fig. 5-19E) goes between them. Shape the top of the back (Fig. 5-20C). Round the top edges of these parts.

Assemble the seat unit with glue and screws. If you decide to cut dovetails or other joints at the corners, allow extra length on the back.

The seat will fit above the central strip (Fig. 5-22A), but do not attach it until you have the parts ready which go under it.

Make the rear axle support to extend ½-inch each side of the seat (Fig. 5-22B). Make packing to go above it with their tops level with the central piece (Fig. 5-22C).

Drill 1½-inch square strips 4-inches long to take the axles (Fig. 5-19F and 22D). These parts are liable to considerable loads. Softwood should be satisfactory, or use a compact hardwood for extra strength. The axles should be a tight fit in their holes.

Glue and screw the axle blocks in place. Join the axle support squarely and centrally to the long piece. Add the packing pieces and then screw on the seat (Fig. 5-19G).

The front axle support (Fig. 5-19H) is a similar size to the rear one, but there is some shaping (Fig. 5-20D). Round the edges of the hollows for the feet. Fit the axle blocks in the same way as those at the rear. Drill holes for the steering rope. The pivot bolt could be ½ inch in diameter. Drill for this and for the alternative positions along the center of the chassis piece.

Make foot guards from ½-inch plywood (Fig. 5-21B and 22E). The curves should be 1 inch larger than the diameter of the wheels. Drill to match the axle blocks. Glue and screw these pieces in place.

Thicken behind the rear axle support with strips each side of the handle slot (Fig. 5-20E and 22F). Drill across for a ⅜-inch pivot bolt. This and the front axle pivot bolt may be carriage bolts secured with washers and locknuts.

Make the handle 36-inches long and put a ½-inch dowel rod through the end as a handle (Fig. 5-19J). Round all edges.

At the inner end of each axle, drill across to take a cotter pin, or bent nail, to prevent the axle pulling out. The outer end will have to be arranged to suit the

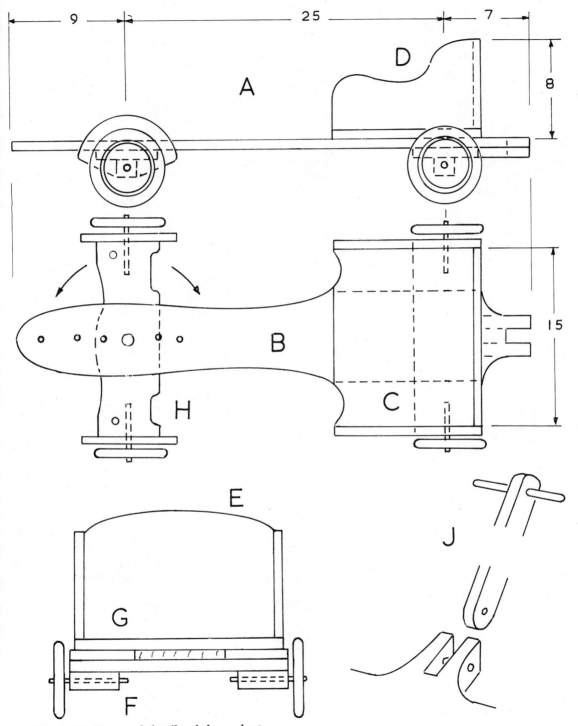

Fig. 5-19. Sizes and details of the go kart.

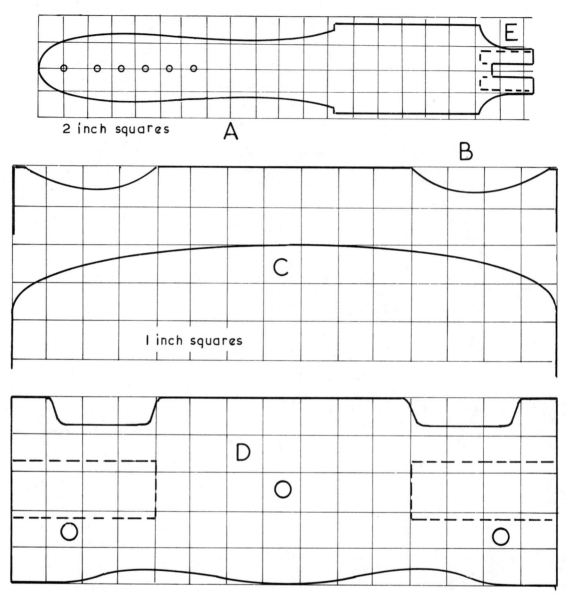

2 inch squares

1 inch squares

Fig. 5-20. Shapes of parts of the go kart.

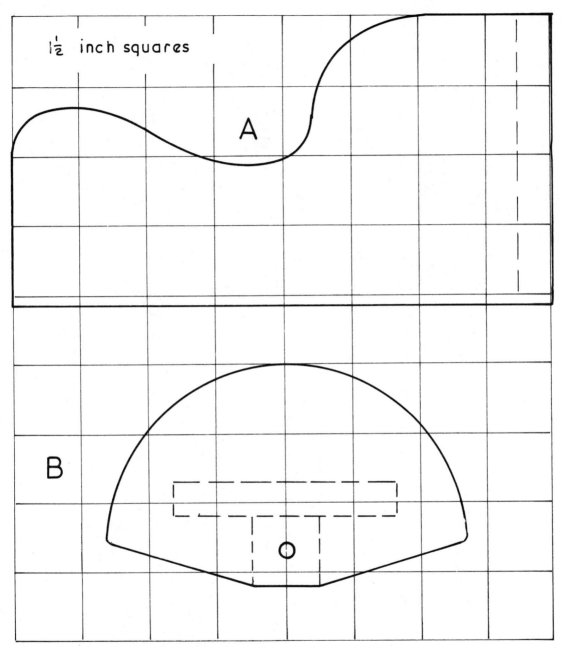

$1\frac{1}{2}$ inch squares

A

B

O

Fig. 5-21. Shapes of more parts for the go kart.

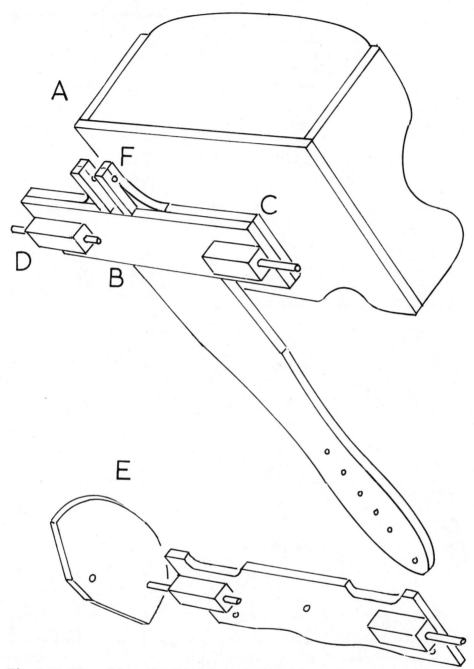

A

F

C

D

B

E

Fig. 5-22. View of the underside of the go kart, showing construction.

wheel and may have another cotter pin. Put one or more washers between the wheel and its supporting block.

Brightly colored paint will be the best finish.

Materials List for Junior Go Kart

1 central member	$\frac{3}{4} \times \quad 7 \times 43$
1 seat bottom	$\frac{3}{4} \times \quad 12 \times 19$
1 seat back	$\frac{3}{4} \times \quad 10 \times 17$
2 seat sides	$\frac{3}{4} \times 7\frac{1}{4} \times 14$
2 axle supports	$\frac{3}{4} \times \quad 5 \times 19$
2 packings	$\frac{3}{4} \times \quad 5 \times 7$
4 axle blocks	$1\frac{1}{2} \times 1\frac{1}{2} \times 6$
2 foot guards	$6 \times \quad 9 \times \frac{1}{2}$ plywood
1 handle	$1 \times \quad 2 \times 38$

Six

Light Furniture

Much furniture made with ordinary shop equipment is often rather severe in its straight lines. A scroll saw allows you to soften and improve the lines by introducing curves. The whole piece of furniture may be formed with curves, but in most cases there are straight lines as well. Modern taste in furniture requires some restraint in embellishment, so do not be carried away by the scope of your scroll saw and overdo the shaping, unless you are making a reproduction of something more appropriate to Victorian days.

Of course, most furniture cannot be made entirely with a scroll saw, but if you obtain wood already finished to width and thickness, it is surprising how much can be done without the aid of other tools. However, most scroll saw users will already be woodworkers with tools for drilling, planing and other processes.

Much use can be made of doweled joints. With prepared dowel rods and suitable drills, you can join your scroll sawn parts. In any case, modern glues are exceptionally strong, but you can depend on glue only between some parts.

In the making of light furniture, as described in this chapter, the scroll saw can be used to cut many joints that might otherwise involve other tools (see Chapter 1). Mortises and tenons make good joints between parts and, in most cases, they can be cut completely with a scroll saw. Dovetails may not seem like work for a scroll saw, but the tails involve straightforward cutting and the sockets can be made by using a tilting table. Finger joints, as at a box corner, may be considered dovetails without the angles; they are straight scroll saw cuts.

Most furniture is made from several pieces of wood joined together. Make sure you understand the entire plan before starting. If you alter the size of one piece of wood, it might not matter, provided that you allow for its effect on other joined parts. This is important regarding thicknesses, particularly if joints are involved. When marking and cutting joints, work on both parts at the same time, even if that means postponing cutting a section, although the rest of a piece of wood has been completed.

Even though you are mainly concerned with curves, check those parts that should be straight really are straight. Also, check that straight edges that should be square with each other are square, even if they are separated by scrolls or other curves. A functional and nicely shaped piece of furniture with scroll saw work is a very satisfying example of your craftsmanship.

CORNER SHELF

This corner shelf may be hung from the walls and will make use of space that might otherwise be empty. The corner shelf (FIG. 6-1) is decorative in itself, and it provides support for a vase of flowers, a potted plant or anything else you may wish to display. A smaller shelf at the top provides stiffness, and it might be used for a little display or may hold one of your souvenirs.

All of the parts are made from ½-inch wood, which may be solid. You could use plywood, if the exposed edges are acceptable. Apply a painted finish to plywood, but a solid hardwood would look best with a clear finish. All of the cutting may be done with a scroll saw. With solid wood, lay out the two sides with their grain vertical, but the two shelves should be cut so the grain runs diagonally to get the maximum strength.

Check the squareness of the corner of the room. If it is close to square you could mark out the shelves with a try square, but if you make the unit square and the corner is appreciably different, there will be an unsightly gap when you mount the unit. If the corner is not square, set an adjustable bevel to the actual angle, and use that to lay out the shelf angles.

Plane the edge of each back straight. Use the squared drawing (FIG. 6-2A) to mark out the pattern. When assembled, one piece has to overlap the other. Cut the two backs at the same time, but tape them together so one edge is ½-inch away from the other (FIG. 6-2B) to allow for the overlapping.

Cut the large shelf to size (FIG. 6-2C). Allow for the actual corner angle if the wall corner is not square.

Check the sizes of the tenons on the shelf against the marked mortises in the back; then cut the mortises.

Do the same with the small shelf (FIG. 6-2D) and its joints.

Drill the backs for hanging screws. It will probably be sufficient to put one screw into each wall under the small top shelf, but you may have to screw lower to find secure attachments in the wall.

Drill for screws between the overlapping backs—#6 × 1¼-inch screws at 4-inch intervals should be satisfactory.

The corner angle between walls is not always sharp, and you might have to round the rear of the unit so the backs will fit closely against both walls.

Sand any exposed edges where necessary, and take sharpness off the angles.

Fig. 6-1. All parts of this corner shelf can be made with a scroll saw.

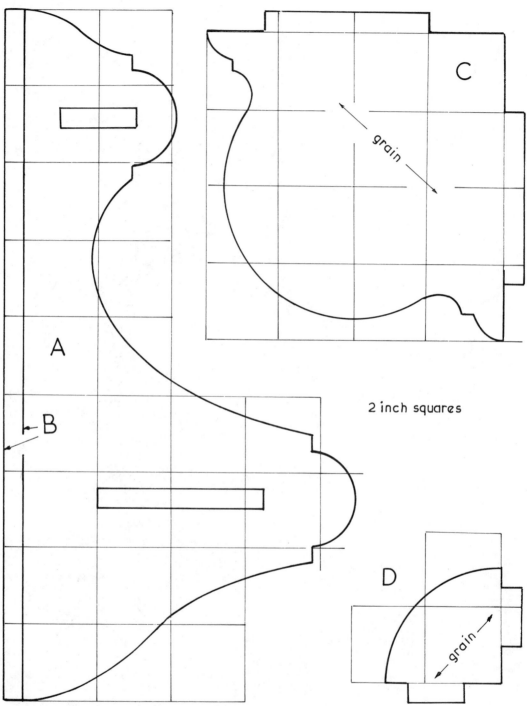

A

B

C

grain

2 inch squares

D

grain

Fig. 6-2. Shapes and sizes of parts of the corner shelf.

Assemble with glue and screws. Level the ends of tenons if they project. Apply your chosen finish and mount the unit.

Materials List for Corner Shelf

2 backs	$\frac{1}{2} \times 9\frac{1}{2} \times 18$
1 shelf	$\frac{1}{2} \times 9\frac{1}{2} \times 12$
1 shelf	$\frac{1}{2} \times 3\frac{1}{2} \times 5$

TAKE-DOWN DISPLAY RACK

This hanging rack (FIG. 6-3) is intended to display plates and souvenirs or other ornaments on two shelves. It is held together with wedges, which make rigid joints. However, if you ever want to take apart the rack and pack it flat, the pieces may be separated.

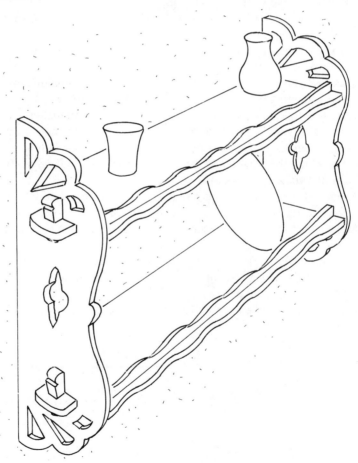

Fig. 6-3. This display rack is wedged together and may be taken apart.

The suggested sizes have the ends 18-inches high and 5-inches wide. The shelves are also 5-inches wide, but you can make them any reasonable length in multiples of 3-inches between the sides, as the edge pattern can be repeated as often as needed. For convenience in the instructions, it is assumed you will make your rack with shelves 21-inches between the sides. In any construction, appearance is best when the dimensions in the three main directions are different. The drawings are based on 1-inch squares, but you could make the rack a different size by drawing your parts on squares of other sizes.

Most parts may be solid wood finished 5/8-inch thick; this gives rigidity without looking too heavy in the sizes suggested. Use a close-grained hardwood, if possible, to give strength in cutout pieces. Use a softwood, if you want to match other furniture, but see that the pieces are without cracks or shakes toward the ends.

Transfer the side shape to one piece of wood (FIG. 6-4A). The top and bottom of each side are the same, with the pattern symmetrical about the center.

Cut the two sides together, but leave the shelf mortises until you have the shelf tenons cut to compare.

Mark out a shelf, arranging the deckle-edge front in 3-inch steps to suit the length you want (FIG. 6-5A).

The wedge holes should finish 1/8-inch inside the thickness of the sides (FIG. 6-5B). Allow for this if you use a different thickness of wood.

Compare the joint parts and cut the mortises in the sides.

It may suit your needs to leave the shelves without the stop pieces along the front edges, but to prevent plates and other items from falling off, the stops are advisable. Make them with the same pattern as the shelf edges (FIG. 6-5C) and a length to fit between the sides.

Make a strip for hanging to go underneath the top shelf (FIG. 6-4B). Drill it for two screws to the wall. Glue this and the front strips to the shelves.

Make a trial assembly. The amount the wedge holes project from the sides will give you a guide to wedge sizes.

Cut four wedges (FIG. 6-4C) slightly too thick. Ease the shelf holes with a file or chisel and maybe take a little off its wedge so each wedge will push in tightly and project the same amount above and below. Check the squareness of the assembly.

Separate the parts, and sand the surfaces and edges. Then finish with paint, or stain and polish.

Materials List for Take-down Display Rack

2 sides	5/8 × 5 × 18
2 shelves	5/8 × 5 × 25
2 stops	1/2 × 5/8 × 22
1 hanging strip	5/8 × 1 × 22
wedges from	5/8 × 3/4 × 10

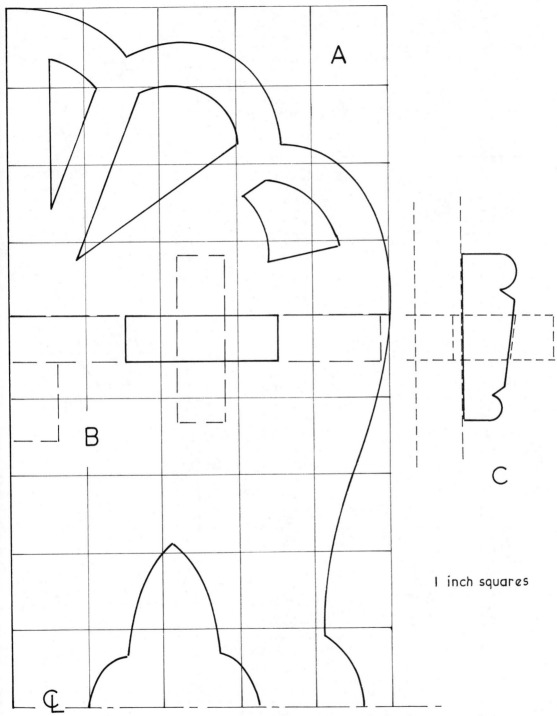

A

B

C

I inch squares

Fig. 6-4. Shapes of the ends and wedges of the display rack.

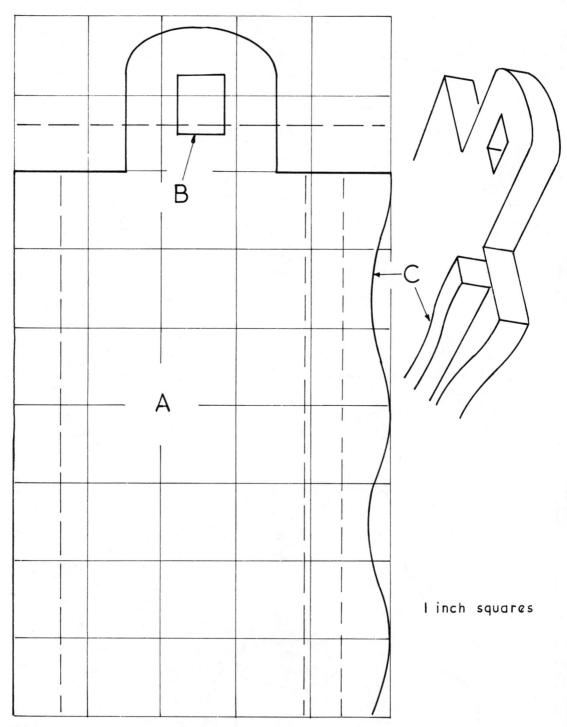

B

A

C

1 inch squares

Fig. 6-5. Shelf details for the display rack.

PLYWOOD COFFEE TABLE

Plywood ¾-inch thick is strong and does not need reinforcing. This coffee table (FIG. 6-6) has legs and top made from that material, with the crossing legs notched into each other and then the top joined to them with strips screwed underneath.

The drawing shows a sea theme, with fish cutouts and the leg edges cut into waves and the top with an edge reminiscent of shells. If you prefer to make your table with smooth edges you can also leave out the fish cutouts, but otherwise make the table in the same way. Suggested sizes are 15-inches high with a top 20-inches across (FIG. 6-7A).

Mark out two sets of legs from the squared drawing (FIG. 6-8). Cut the central notch in one piece at the top and the other at the bottom (FIG. 6-7B), making these a close fit on the plywood.

Fig. 6-6. All parts of this coffee table are plywood.

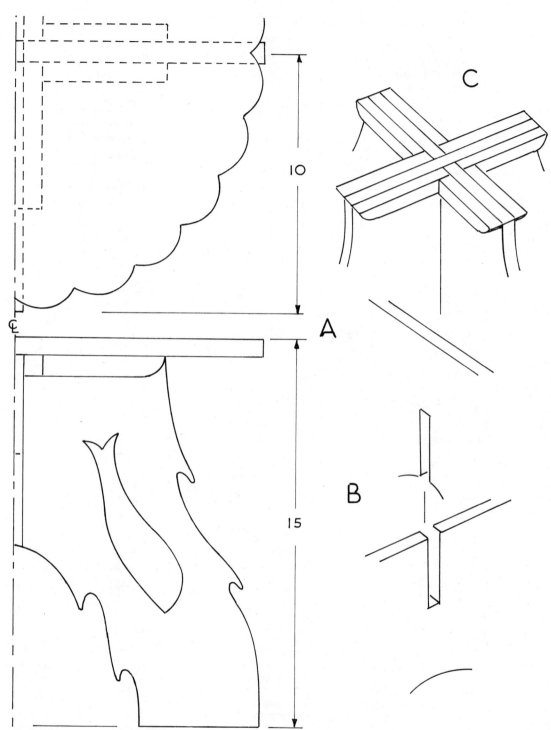

Fig. 6-7. Sizes and construction of the plywood coffee table.

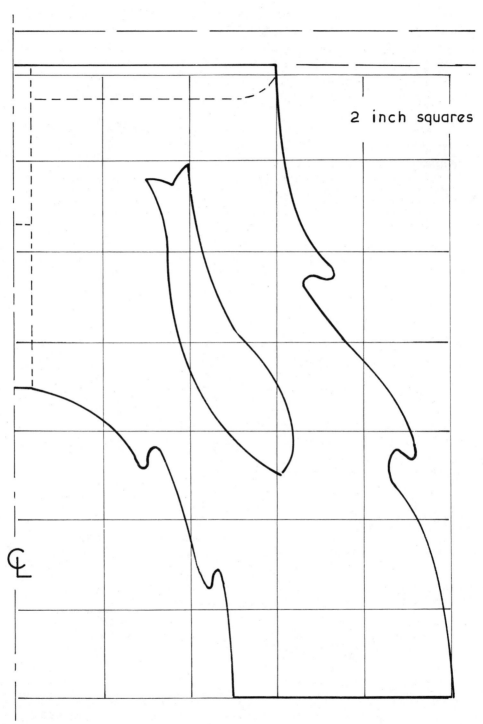

2 inch squares

Fig. 6-8. Shape of a leg of the coffee table.

Mark the plywood for the top with two lines crossing squarely. Use the quarter drawing (FIG. 6-9A) to mark one quarter of the rim at a time. A hardboard template will ensure uniformity. It is helpful in matching the sections if you make the template with one extra pattern (FIG. 6-9B).

Sand edges where necessary and remove any sharp corners.

Prepare wood for the top joints (FIG. 6-7C). Round the outer ends. Drill for screws into the plywood both ways.

Glue the notched legs to each other; then, glue and screw the square strips to the top edges. Check that the crossing is square. When the glue has set, level the top surfaces.

Mark the leg positions on the inverted top; then, glue and screw on the leg assembly.

Check that the table stands without wobbling on a level surface. If necessary, plane a foot.

If you have used hardwood plywood, you may choose a stain and a clear finish. Softwood plywood is better painted.

Materials List for Plywood Coffee Table

2 legs	$3/4 \times 10 \times 15$ plywood
1 top	$3/4 \times 21 \times 21$ plywood
8 joints	$3/4 \times 3/4 \times 7$

FOOT STOOL

A small stool can have many uses in a home: as a child's seat, a means of reaching higher, or as a foot stool. This project (FIG. 6-10) is proportioned as a foot stool, but it will serve for many other purposes. You could alter the sizes. Be careful that the top does not overhang the spread of the legs very much, so there is little risk of a load near an edge tipping the stool.

As drawn (FIG. 6-11), the stool is intended to be made throughout of wood finished $3/4$-inch thick. This gives weight and stability, but you could reduce the thicknesses a little if you wish. You could use hardwood and give the stool a stained and polished finish, but painted softwood would be appropriate. With the deckle edge pattern, bright colors would give the stool a gypsy finish, particularly if you paint the legs a different color from the top. If you want to use the stool for standing on, avoid too high a gloss finish on the top.

The sizes (FIG. 6-11A) may be regarded as the basic straight line pattern; then the decoration is $3/4$-inch outside that. Setting out is straightforward, except you need to know the angle to make the legs. Lay this out (FIG. 6-11B), and set an adjustable bevel to the angle for marking cuts on the legs. The curves which decorate the top and sides are mostly the same. It will help in keeping the curves uniform if you make a hardboard, or card, template of two adjoining curves. In this way, you can move it along to mark as many of the curves as required.

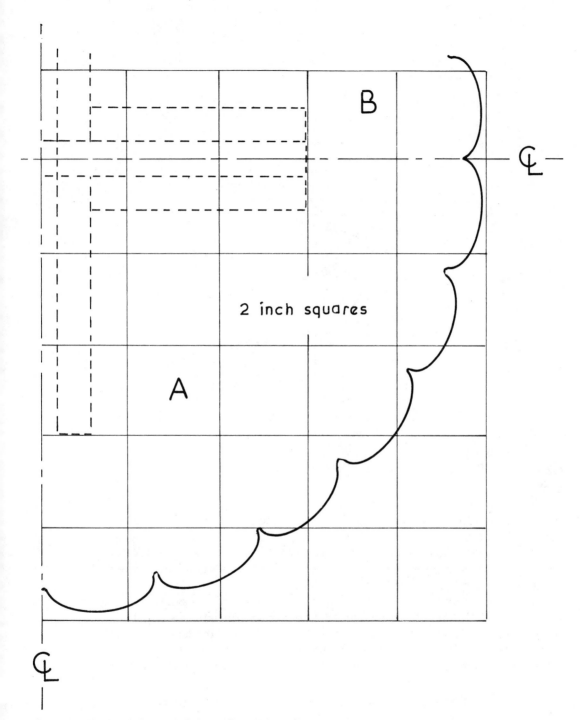

Fig. 6-9. Shape of the top of the coffee table.

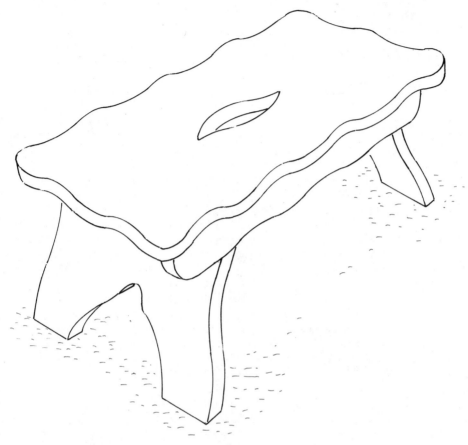

Fig. 6-10. A strong foot stool with a lifting hand hole.

Mark out the top (FIG. 6-11C) and locate on its underside the positions of the side pieces and the tops of the legs. Draw the edge pattern (FIG. 6-12A) evenly outside the marks of the other pieces.

A hand hole is suggested (FIG. 6-12B). This is optional; leave it out or use your own design. Decorate the center of the stool with cutout initials or another pattern, but do not arrange very large holes in the top.

Make the two sides (FIG. 6-11D). The curves along the edge are similar to those on the top, but the ends are curved up so there is a short length of straight edge where each leg will fit (FIG. 6-12C). Mark on the positions of the legs.

Cut these pieces to shape. Take the sharpness off the shaped edges of the sides, but round the edges of the top to make a comfortable grip. Round the edges of the hand hole.

Lay out the shapes of the legs (FIG. 6-11E). Allow for the beveled ends (FIG. 6-12D).

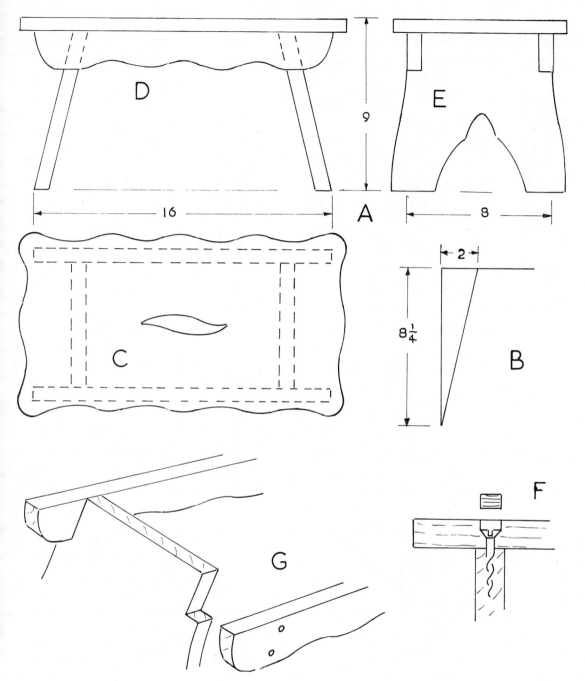

Fig. 6-11. Sizes and construction of the foot stool.

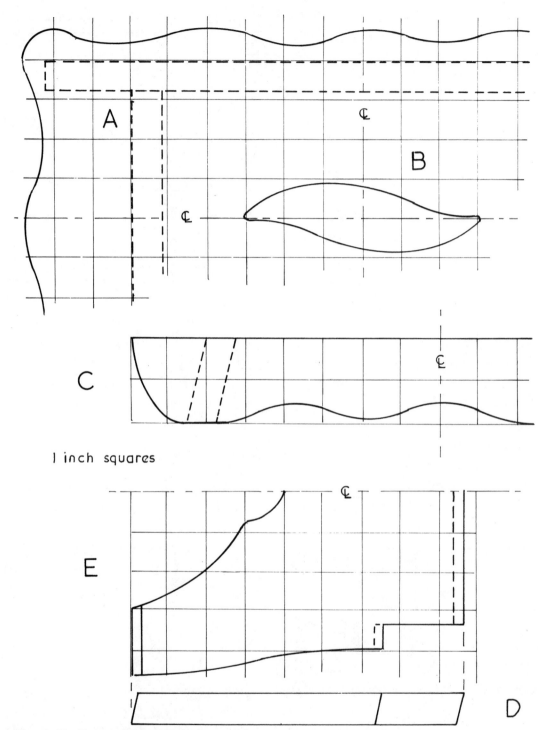

A

B

℄

℄

C

1 inch squares

E

℄

℄

D

Fig. 6-12. Shapes of parts of the foot stool.

Make the notches to match the depths of the sides. Cut the legs to shape (FIG. 6-12E) and check their fit and angles against the sides.

You can use glue in the joints, but screws will pull the parts together. You might countersink the screws level with the surfaces, but it will be better to counterbore and cover the screw heads with plugs (FIG. 6-11F). Use two #8 gauge $\times 1\frac{1}{2}$- or 2-inch screws at each joint between a leg and a side (FIG. 6-11G). For a clear finish, consider using plugs of a different color wood from the main parts, so when you have planed the plugs level they make a contrasting pattern of round dots.

Check the leg and side assemblies for squareness, and see that they stand level. If necessary, plane the top surfaces level.

Try the top in position. Mark for screws at about 4-inch intervals; then, drill and counterbore for screws into the sides.

Sand all over and apply your chosen finish.

Materials List for Foot Stool

1 top	$\frac{3}{4} \times 9\frac{1}{2} \times 19$
2 sides	$\frac{3}{4} \times \quad 2 \times 18$
2 legs	$\frac{3}{4} \times 9\frac{1}{2} \times 10$

OUTLINED BRACKETED SHELVES

Plain shelves with straight lines may be all that are needed in a shop or garage, but for most of the rooms in the house they can look better if they are shaped so that straight lines are few. This is where the user of a scroll saw has an advantage. You can cut curves as easily as straight lines. A shelf can be made to be supported by a single bracket, or you can make it longer with two or more brackets.

It is possible to make a shelf unit with internal frets, as in the following project, but for this project there are no internal ornamental cuts to be made. The outlines are related between the parts, and they are based on architectural forms (FIG. 6-13). The first drawings suit a unit with a back 8-inches high and 14-inches long, from which the shelf projects 5 inches. However, if you choose squares bigger or smaller than 1 inch when setting out, you can alter the overall sizes. Instructions for converting the design to a unit twice as long follow the instructions for a single bracket shelf (FIG. 6-13A).

Solid wood may be used, and all parts should be finished $\frac{5}{8}$-inch thick. The unit would look attractive in a good hardwood to match other furniture in the room, probably with a stained and polished finish, but painted softwood would be appropriate in some situations.

Mark out the back (FIG. 6-14A) symmetrically about a vertical centerline. Mark the mortises to suit the actual thickness of the wood for the other parts. Cut the outline, but leave cutting the mortises until you can check them against other parts.

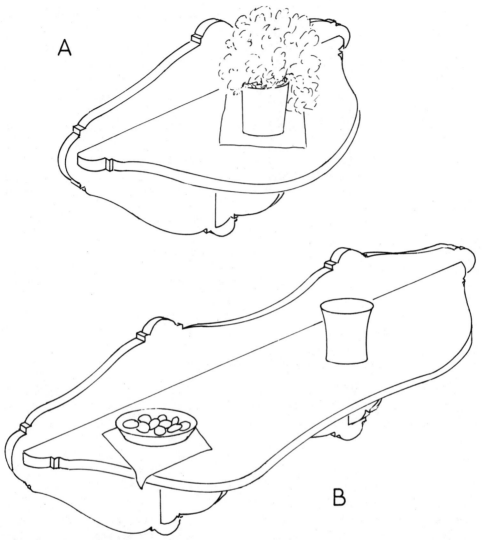

A

B

Fig. 6-13. Two versions of outlined bracketed shelves.

Mark and cut the outline of the shelf (FIG. 6-15A) in the same way.

If possible, cut the bracket (FIG. 6-15B) with its grain running diagonally (FIG. 6-15C) for maximum strength. Be careful that the corner angle does not finish less than 90 degrees, as this would cause the shelf to tilt forward slightly. It would be safer to have the angle a degree or so greater.

Check the bracket tenon against the mortise on the back, and cut that to match.

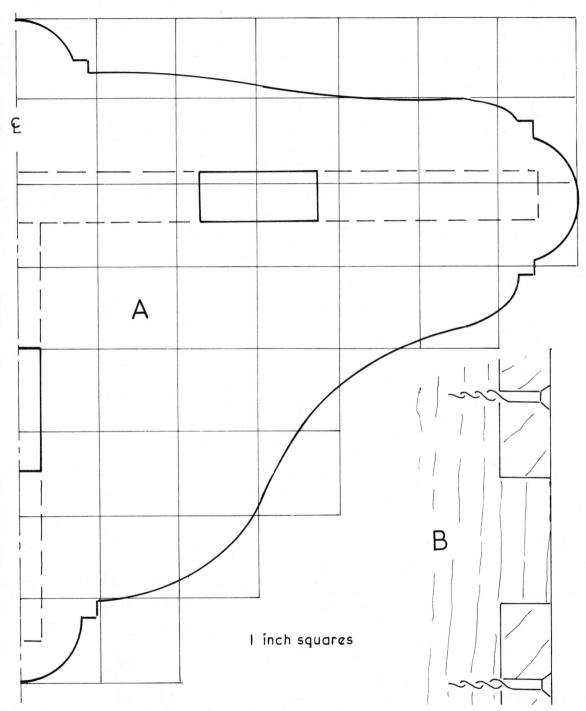

3

A

B

1 inch squares

Fig. 6-14. Shape of the back of a bracketed shelf.

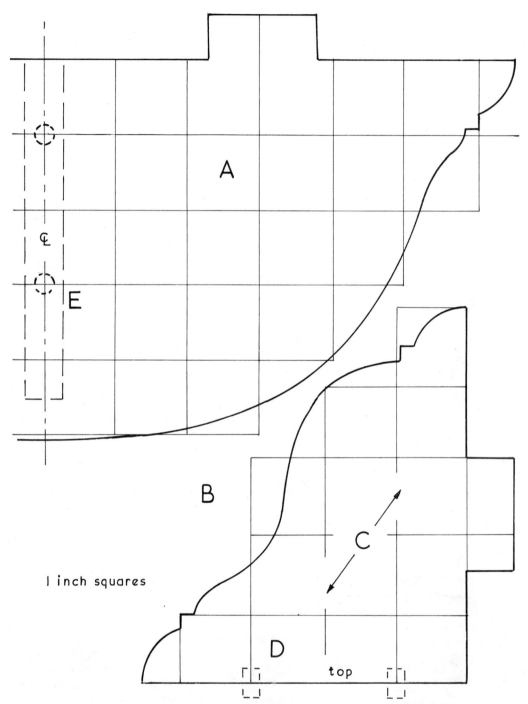

A

C̶L

E

1 inch squares

B

C

D

top

Fig. 6-15. The shapes of a shelf and its brackets.

With the bracket temporarily in position, check the mortise positions in relation to the shelf tenons. The shelf has to fit closely against the bracket. Cut these mortises.

The mortises locate the parts, but strength comes from screws driven through the back into the shelf and bracket edges. It should be sufficient to drill for screws a short distance each side of the mortises (FIG. 6-14B).

To secure the shelf to the bracket without screw heads showing on top, use two ¼-inch dowels (FIG. 6-15D) with matching holes under the shelves (FIG. 6-15E).

Do any necessary sanding, but rounding edges should not be necessary, as the angular sections emphasize the curved outlines. Assemble with glue and screws; then apply your chosen finish.

The neatest way to mount the unit on the wall is with two screws positioned about ½ inch under the shelf and a short distance in from the ends.

If you wish to make a longer unit with two brackets, the general methods of construction are the same as for the single-bracket unit with the following exceptions.

The two-bracket shelf unit (FIG. 6-13B) is about twice as long as the single unit, but other sizes are the same. You could make the unit a few inches longer or shorter by varying the amount between the two sections.

Make the back (FIG. 6-16A) symmetrical about the centerline. The parts outside the bracket positions are the same as the single unit, but between them the patterns blend into each other. Mark the mortises, but do not cut them until the other parts can be checked against them. Cut the outline.

Mark out and cut the shelf completely (FIG. 6-16B). Mark the bracket positions on the underside.

Mark and cut two brackets the same as for the single unit (FIG. 6-15B).

Check the bracket and shelf tenons against the mortise positions on the back. Cut the mortises to fit.

Prepare for dowels (FIG. 6-15D) between the brackets and the underside of the shelf and drill for screws through the back into the shelf and brackets.

Try a dry assembly. If this is satisfactory, sand where necessary, then assemble with glue, screws and dowels.

Drill for screws to the wall in similar positions to those suggested for the single-bracketed shelf. Apply your chosen finish.

Materials List for Outlined Bracketed Shelves

Single-bracket shelf		
1 back	⅝ ×	8 × 16
1 shelf	⅝ ×	6 × 15
1 bracket	⅝ × 4½ ×	8
Double-bracket shelf		
1 back	⅝ ×	8 × 28
1 shelf	⅝ ×	8 × 27
2 brackets	⅝ × 4½ ×	8

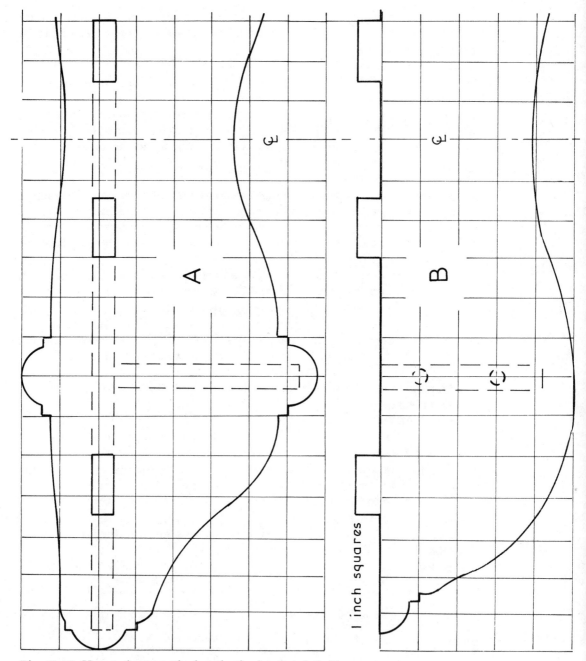

A

B

ᴇ

ᴇ

1 inch squares

Fig. 6-16. How to increase the length of a bracketed shelf.

FRETTED BRACKETED SHELF

You can add to the interest and decoration of a bracketed shelf by making internal cuts as well as external ones. The shelf (FIG. 6-17) is made in the same way as the single-bracketed shelf in the previous project, but the bracket and back are decorated by fretted cuts, giving you scope to show your skill with the scroll saw.

The unit may be made of wood ⅝-inch thick. Painting would take some of the sharpness off the finger cuts and your work might lose some of its effect, so it is better to apply a clear finish. Use enough to seal the wood, but not enough to build up a high gloss.

Many patterns are possible. If you prepare your own, it is best to arrange the amount to be cut out to be less than the wood that is left and to avoid leaving narrow parts, particularly across the grain. Some suggested designs are offered (FIGS. 6-19 and 20). These are arranged so the top edge is 4 inches and the upright edge is 5 inches. You will have to allow for a tenon on the upright edge. Whatever the design, allow enough solid wood along the edges to take screws or dowels.

Mark out a bracket to the chosen design, but with a tenon and positions for dowels similar to the previous project (FIG. 6-15B, C and D). Cut it to shape, including all internal cuts.

Mark out the back (FIG. 6-18C) with the two patterns the same as the brackets, with a 1-inch width between them. Mark on the positions of the shelf and the bracket. If you want a ledge above the shelf line, allow up to 1-inch there. If you

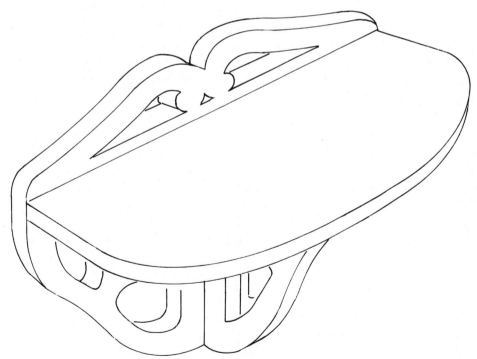

Fig. 6-17. A shelf with fretted back and bracket.

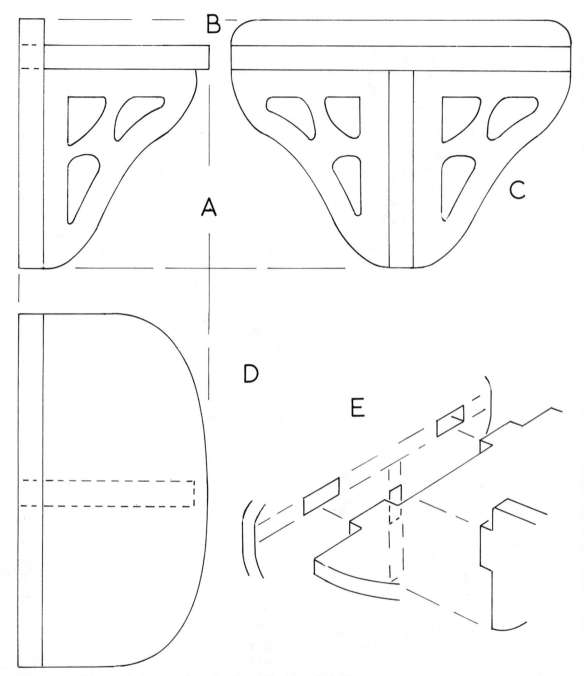

Fig. 6-18. Parts and construction of a fretted bracketed shelf.

Fig. 6-19. Other designs for use in the fretted bracketed shelf.

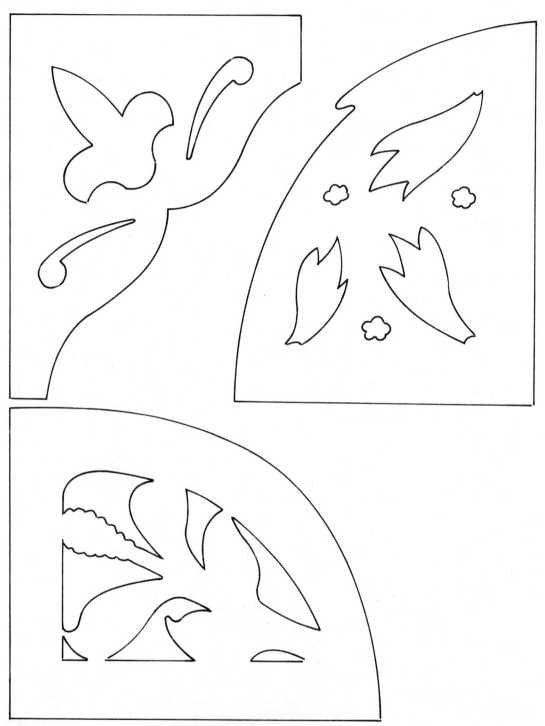

Fig. 6-20. More possible designs for the fretted bracketed shelf.

want a shaped and fretted top, mark the pattern (FIG. 6-21A) symmetrical about a centerline. Cut the back to shape, but leave the mortises until you can check tenons on the other parts against them.

The shelf could be made with square or beveled corners. Lightly round corners if you want maximum shelf space, but the suggested outline is fully curved (FIGS. 6-18D and 21B). Allow for two tenons on the rear edge.

Use the shelf and bracket to check positions for mortises in the back, and cut them (FIG. 6-18E).

Prepare the top edge of the bracket and the shelf for two ¼-inch dowels.

Drill for screws from the back into the shelf and the bracket (FIG. 6-14B).

Do any sanding or other final work; then, assemble the unit with glue and screws. The least conspicuous place for screws to the wall is about ½-inch below the shelf, and a short distance in from each end. Apply your chosen finish.

Materials List for Fretted Bracketed Shelf

1 back	⅝ × 6 or 7 × 10
1 shelf	⅝ × 5 × 10
1 bracket	⅝ × 4 × 6

MAGAZINE RACK

A rack or bin to hold newspapers and magazines provides scope for the scroll saw, as most of the parts involve curves or other cuts that are best made with this tool. This project (FIG. 6-22) is a portable rack which will hold a large amount of reading matter and is convenient to have at the side of a chair. It could also be used for knitting or sewing work.

The rack is designed to be made of ⅜-inch (9mm) plywood. The exposed edges of a hardwood plywood may be regarded as a decorative feature. You could vary the thickness of plywood. The central piece with the handle could be ½-inch thick and the outer parts ¼-inch thick. Using ½-inch plywood throughout is possible, but the rack would be heavy in appearance and in fact.

Most parts are joined with mortise and tenon joints, with the tenons projecting through with rounded ends. Only the bottom need be pinned. If you cut the joints to a good fit, glue should be all that is needed to hold the parts together. If necessary, drive a few pins through the sides into the ends; then, set them below the surface and cover the heads with wood filler.

Mark out and cut the two ends first (FIG. 6-23A), and use them to check sizes of other parts that connect to them. All mortises and tenons are 2-inches wide. Tenons on the sides of the ends should be cut square to the slopes, not parallel with the bottom. Keep rounding of the ends of tenons outside the thickness of the plywood they will penetrate.

Mark out and cut the bottom (FIG. 6-23B). Bevel the edges to match the slopes of the sides, but be careful not to make the bottom too narrow — with the tenons through the ends the edges of the parts should match.

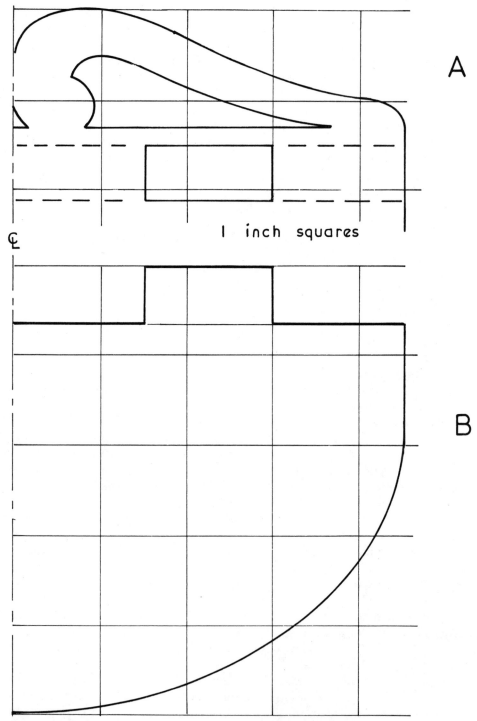

A

℄

1 inch squares

B

Fig. 6-21. Patterns for a top and the shelf of a fretted bracketed shelf.

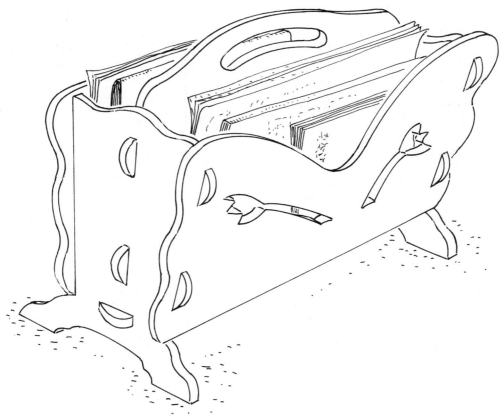

Fig. 6-22. A magazine rack with the main parts tenoned together.

Make the central division (FIG. 6-24A) the same length as the bottom. See that the tenons match the end mortises (FIG. 6-24B) and the lower edge will rest on the bottom.

Well round the exposed part of the handle and the hand hole. Other exposed parts in the finished rack will probably look better left square in section, except for sharpness taken off the edges.

The pair of sides provide most of the decoration in the rack. If you prefer a plainer finish, you can modify the outline and leave out the pierced designs. Mark symmetrically about the centerline (FIG. 6-25A). Check the spacing between the mortises with the parts already made. Note that the lower edge projects below the rack bottom (FIG. 6-25B).

You may find it easier to assemble in two stages. Join the bottom to the division with glue and a few pins; then, join these parts to the end. Let the glue set in these joints.

Glue on the two sides, and use a few pins into the edges of the rack bottom. If the tenons are not as good a fit in the mortises in the sides as you wished, they

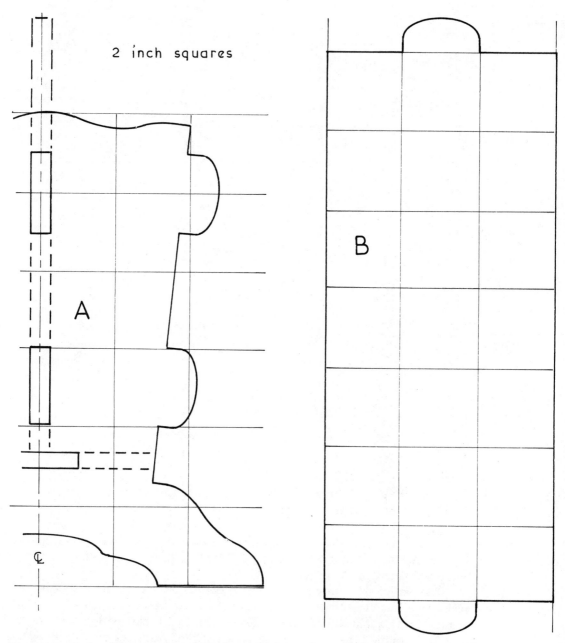

2 inch squares

A

B

C

Fig. 6-23. End and bottom shapes for the magazine rack.

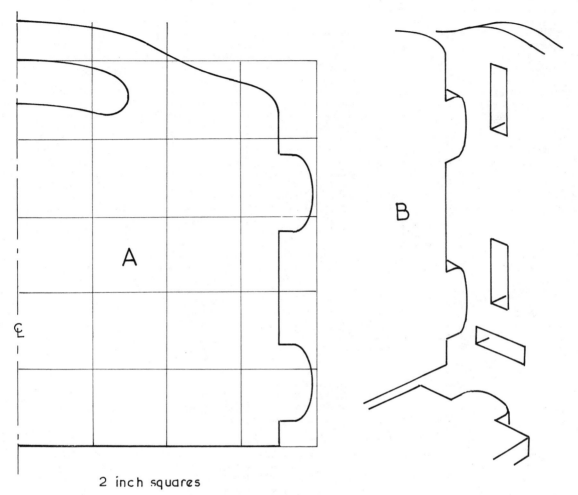

2 inch squares

Fig. 6-24. The central division of the magazine rack. The way parts fit into the ends.

could be supplemented with pins near the top edges, where most strain can be expected to come.

Remove any surplus glue and apply a clear finish, over stain, if you wish.

Materials List for Magazine Rack

(3/4-inch plywood)
2 ends	12 × 14
1 division	12 × 18
1 bottom	6 × 18
2 sides	10 × 10

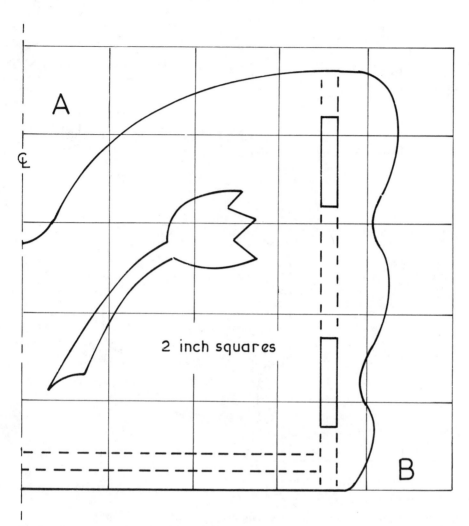

A

C̵L

2 inch squares

B

Fig. 6-25. Pattern for the sides of the magazine rack.

Seven

Large Furniture

A modern scroll saw has a capacity for cutting very thick wood compared with earlier fretwork machines that were only satisfactory cutting up to ½ inch or so. The thickness of the possible cut varies between the makes and sizes of the machine, but if you want to make use of your full capacity you can choose fairly ambitious projects.

An advantage of using a scroll saw for cuts that might also be done with a bandsaw or other tool is that a scroll saw blade leaves a finish that may need little or no treatment, while a bandsaw or jigsaw cut will finish rather rough.

Cuts on thick wood may be slow. You must let the saw cut at its own speed without forcing the wood hard against it; then you will get good edges. Be patient. Making furniture with thicker wood can be very satisfying, and it will show you that the tool is capable of much more than traditional fretwork.

The projects in this chapter are not necessarily larger than those in Chapter 6, but they involve cuts in thicker wood, with some of it up to the capacity of the machine. Thick wood should be dry. Wood that is insufficiently seasoned or is resinous might stick to the saw. In general, softwoods should be easier to cut than hardwoods, but many seasoned hardwoods cut well, and they will produce the cleanest lines, particularly in fine details.

PEDESTAL SIDE TABLE

The wood for a fullsize dining table would be too thick to be shaped by a scroll saw, but it is possible to make a side table with the appearance of a traditional type of dining table, using wood 1-inch thick; although, if your machine has a greater thickness capacity and you are prepared for the slower work, you could increase the wood thickness by up to ¼ inch.

The wood required is all 1-inch thick, and the only very wide part is the top, which will have to be made by gluing boards together. Hardwood to match existing furniture would be a good choice, but painted softwood might be acceptable in some situations and would be easier to cut. Overall sizes of parts should suit most machines, but otherwise you might have to mount a blade crosswise for some cuts in a more restricted machine.

The table (FIG. 7-1) has two pedestals joined by two main rails with wedged tenons; then, there are two narrower rails under the top (FIG. 7-2 and 3). This arrangement gives ample rigidity, despite the comparatively light wood sections.

The recommended sequence of work is to make and assemble the two pedestals; then, make and fit the rails. Finally, add the top.

Fig. 7-1. A pedestal side table.

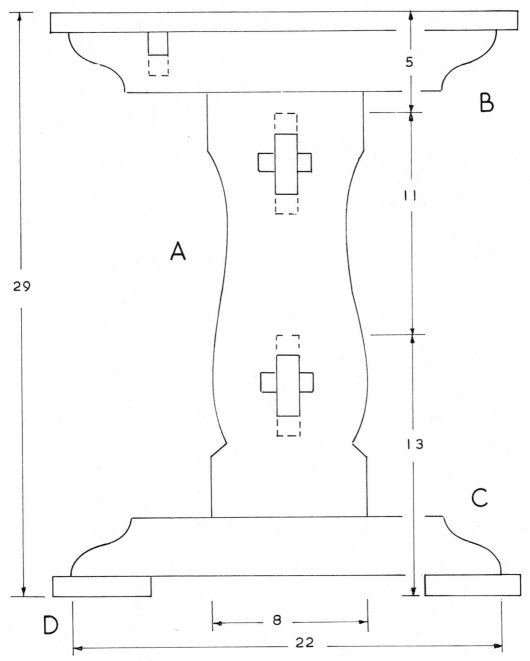

Fig. 7-2. Sizes of an end of the pedestal side table.

Mark and shape the pair of uprights (FIG. 7-2A and 4A). cut the curved outlines and see that the ends are square, or the pedestals will not finish upright. The mortises may be left until you have cut the tenons to fit them.

The top and bottom of the pedestals (FIG. 7-2B and C) are the same, except for the notches in the top rails. Mark and cut their ends (FIG. 7-4B). The notches in the top parts (FIG. 7-4C and 5A) are to take the top rails.

Mark and drill these parts for ½-inch dowels (FIG. 7-5B). Four in each position should be sufficient. Assemble these parts. Check that they are square and the pair match.

Make feet (FIG. 7-2C and 5C) to extend 1 inch on each side. Round the corners and edges. Join with glue and screws from below.

The top rails reach the outsides of the pedestals, but the lower rails extend through 2½ inches. Make sure all rails have the same distances between shoulders.

Make the two top rails (FIG. 7-3A and 5D). Notch the ends to fit the pedestal tops, and cut the lower edges to a wavy outline (FIG. 7-4D).

Make the two lower rails (FIG. 7-3B and 5E) with tenons to match the mortises and wavy edges similar to those on the top rails (FIG. 7-4E). Mark the positions of the wedge holes and the curve of the ends, but leave cutting these until after you have fitted the wedges.

Make four wedges (FIG. 7-4F and 5F). Cut them too long and mark, but do not yet cut the curved tops.

So the wedge will pull a joint tight, its slot has to be cut about ⅛-inch below the surface of the pedestal (FIG. 7-4G). Mark this and cut the hole, so when a wedge is driven in it pulls the joint tight without touching the bottom of the hole. Bevel the outer edge of the square hole to match the slope of the wedge.

When you are satisfied with the fit of the wedges, mark them so each projects the same amount each side of the tenons. Then, shape the curved top and remove any projecting sharp edges.

Glue boards to make up the width of the top. If you would have difficulty in manipulating the complete top in your scroll saw to cut the corners (FIG. 7-3C and 4H), you might find it easier to prepare the parts for gluing. Then, cut the corners on the outside pieces before joining.

The top may be attached to the framework with pocket screws (FIG. 7-5G). It should be sufficient to locate a screw inside each pedestal top about 2-inches in from its end, and two more inside each top rail, so the top is held by glue and eight screws. Prepare the parts for screws, either by cutting the slots with a gouge or chisel, or with a Forstner bit.

Wedge the bottom rails in place. It will be better to do this without glue, then any later slackness due to shrinking can be taken up.

Glue the top rails in place. Strengthen each joint by driving a screw down through it, if you wish.

Check that the assembly is square and stands upright on a level surface.

Invert the assembly on the underside of the top. Locate it centrally (FIG. 7-3D); then screw it on. Unless the wood is very stable, the top will be liable to expand

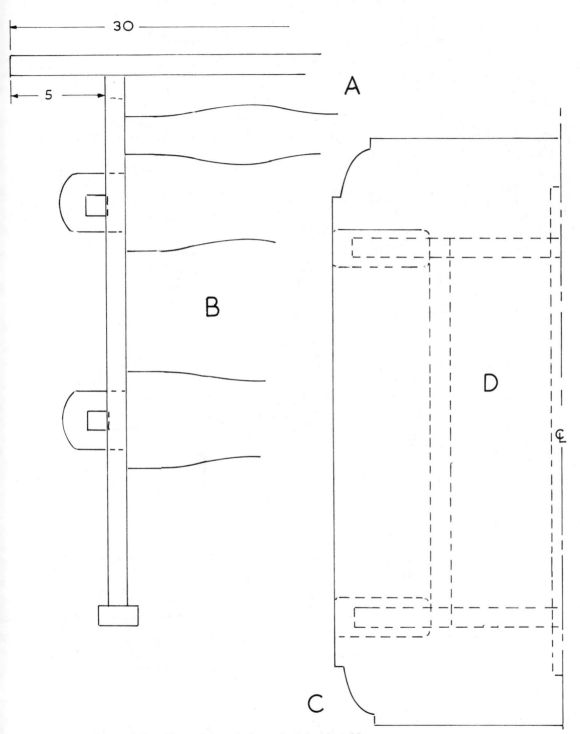

Fig. 7-3. Views of the side and top of the pedestal side table.

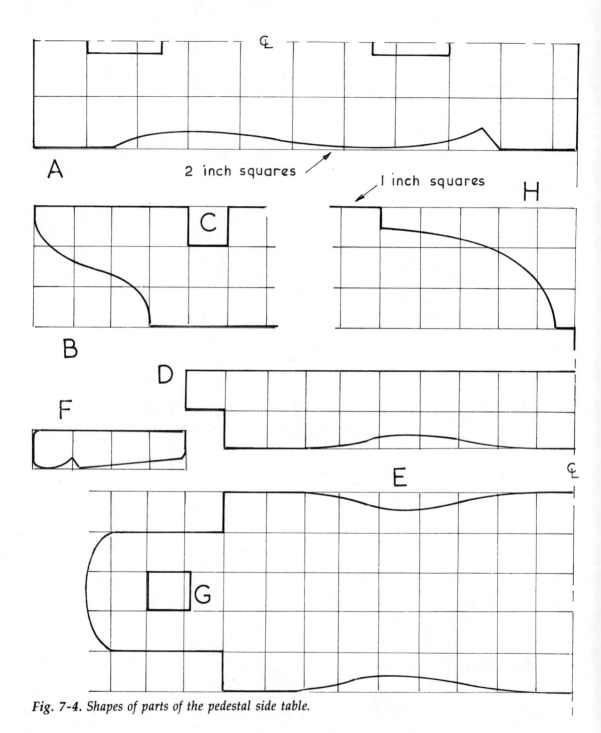

A

2 inch squares

1 inch squares

H

C

B

D

F

E

G

Fig. 7-4. Shapes of parts of the pedestal side table.

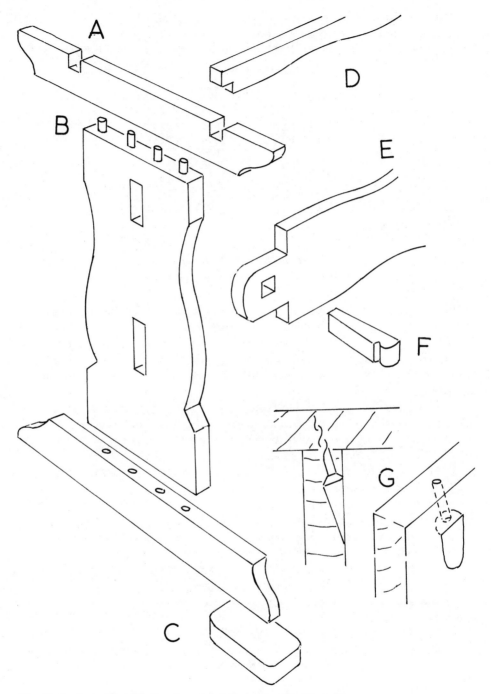

Fig. 7-5. Assembly details of parts of the pedestal side table.

and contract a little. If you use screws without glue, this should allow slight movement without the risk of splitting.

If this assembly is satisfactory, you might wish to remove the top for final sanding of all parts, followed by application of stain and polish.

Materials List for Pedestal Side Table

2 uprights	1 × 8 × 23
4 pedestal ends	1 × 3 × 24
4 feet	1 × 2 × 7
2 top rails	1 × 2 × 22
2 lower rails	1 × 5 × 27
wedges from	1 × 1 × 20
1 top	1 × 24 × 32

JACOBEAN STOOL

A form of stylized animal leg was popular on a lot of furniture of earlier years. This *cabriole* leg terminated in a paw or a claw holding a ball. Some legs were elaborately carved. The style reached its peak during the Jacobean period.

You could carve legs in this way, but for modern furniture, shaped legs with cleaner lines are preferable. This stool (FIG. 7-6) has cabriole legs of square section. Although, you could round the lower parts, if you wish, to give a better representation of a paw. The legs are joined with deep rails and there is a lift-out upholstered top.

The legs are cut from 2½-inch square stock. If that is more than the capacity of your scroll saw, reduce the section by easing the curves to be cut, but too much reduction of section would spoil the affect. A furniture-quality hardwood is advised. This is not a project for softwood.

The design (FIG. 7-7) is for a 17-inch square tool, 14-inches high. The sizes could be altered by several inches without affecting the method of construction.

You must mark the outlines of the leg eight times, and you will need to check your work, so make a template from hardboard or thin plywood first (FIG. 7-8A).

Mark the shapes of the legs on two adjoining faces of each piece of 2½-inch square wood, but do not cut the shapes yet.

Mark the four rails (FIG. 7-7A and 8B). See that they are all the same size and the ends are square. Cut the shaped lower edges.

Glue and pin ½-inch square strips in place ½-inch down from each rail top edge (FIG. 7-9A).

Mark the ends for three ½-inch dowels (FIG. 7-8C).

Mark the legs for matching dowel holes (FIG. 7-9B). The ½-inch strips should come level with the inner corners of the legs (FIG. 7-9C). Drill the dowel holes. Allow for the dowels going ¾ inch into each part.

Saw the legs to shape. Cut the pattern one way on a leg; then use adhesive tape to hold the pieces cut away in position while you cut the same outline the

Fig. 7-6. A Jacobean stool with upholstered top and modified cabriole legs.

other way. Use your template to check shapes and do any necessary corrections and sanding.

Cut out the inner corners of the tops of the legs to match where the ½-inch strips will meet them (FIG. 7-9D), so there will be a clear square opening for the lift-out top.

Glue and dowel the parts together. Assemble the opposite sides squarely and let their glue set; then, add the rails the other way. Check squareness from above and at the sides. Stand back and look at the assembly to check its appearance on a level surface.

The top may be made with plastic or rubber foam about 1½-inch thick, covered with cloth and tacked onto a piece of ½-inch plywood. Cut the plywood base to size. How much clearance you allow in the stool depends on the thickness of the covering cloth. You have to be able to lift out the top, but it should make a push fit rather than a loose one (FIG. 7-7B).

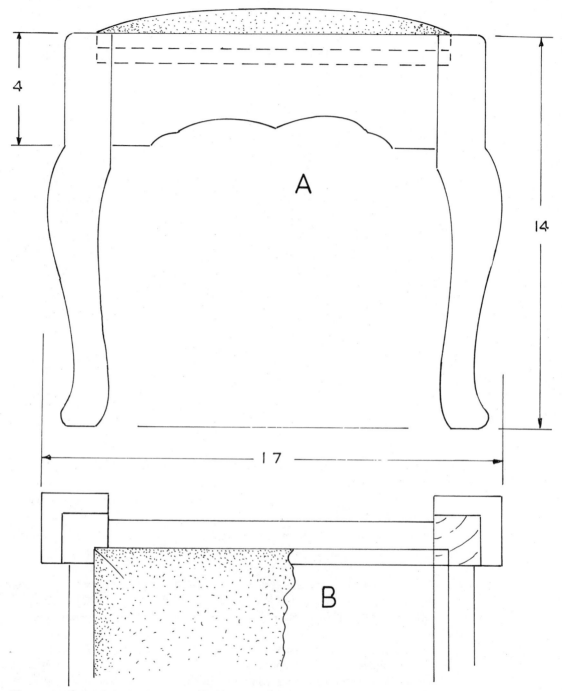

Fig. 7-7. Sizes of the Jacobean stool.

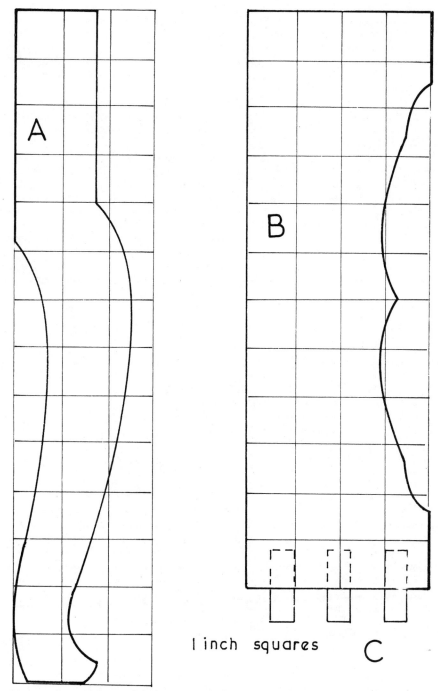

Fig. 7-8. Shapes of the leg and rail for the Jacobean stool.

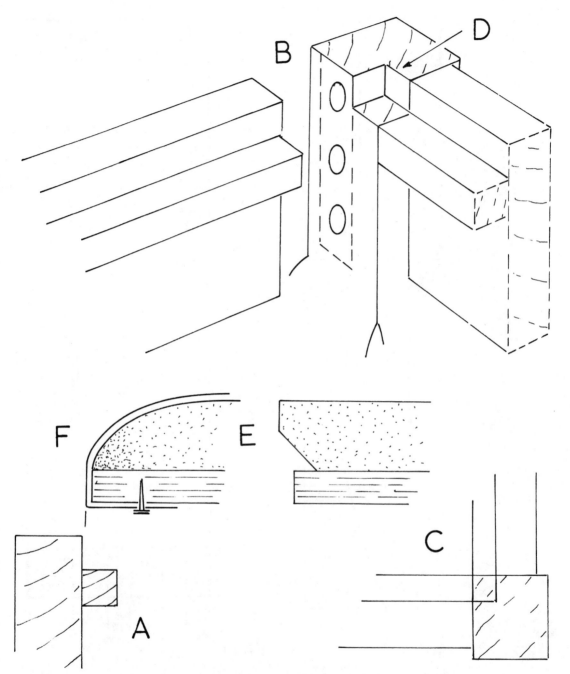

Fig. 7-9. *Details of a corner and the upholstery of the Jacobean stool.*

Drill a pattern of four or five ½-inch holes in the base to let air in and out.

Cut the foam about ¼-inch too big all round, and bevel the lower edges (FIG. 7-9E). This allows the foam edges to be compressed, so the hard edge of the plywood does not show through the cloth.

Cut the cloth with plenty to spare. Use ⅜-inch tacks to fix it. Have the top assembly inverted, and pull the cloth from opposite sides to tighten and compress the foam. Tack far enough in to be clear of the supporting strips (FIG. 7-9F).

Work from the center of each side outwards towards the corners with tacks. How close you put them depends on the foam and the cloth, but 1½-inch spacing is a guideline.

At each corner, pull the cloth to overlap and tack. Cut away any surplus while doing this. Remove any excess cloth. It is the appearance of the cloth on the top which matters. Trim the cloth edges inside the line of tacks.

Round the outer edges and corners of the tops of the legs. Take sharpness off any other exposed edges on the stool. Sand thoroughly; then finish with stain and polish.

Materials List for Jacobean Stool

4 legs	2½ × 2½ × 16
4 rails	1 × 4 × 14
4 strips	½ × ½ × 14
1 top	15 × 15 × ½ plywood

TELEPHONE WALL UNIT

This unit (FIG. 7-10) is intended to screw to a wall and provide all the accommodation needed for a telephone, together with plenty of space for directories and other papers, with a drop-down flap for writing on. Also you can store magazines and many different types of answering machines.

Construction is with wood ¾-inch thick; in most situations, this would be a hardwood to match other furniture. Assembly of the main parts is with ⅜-inch dowels, but for the neatest finish at the back, the rear edges of the sides are rabbeted to take plywood. You may need to check sizes of your local telephone directories, but the shelves are drawn large enough to take most magazines, so there should be ample room as specified (FIG. 7-11A).

Mark out the pair of sides first (FIG. 7-11B and 12A). Locate the positions of other parts. Rabbet for the plywood back and deepen the rabbet above the top shelf line for the upper back (FIG. 7-13A). Note that the drop-down flap is set back from the front edge. Cut the shaped ends and the hollowed front edges.

Make the top and bottom shelves, which are the same (FIG. 7-11C). The curved front edges (FIG. 7-12B) project about 2-inches in front of the sides. Round these edges in section.

The other shelf is parallel and extends to just inside the drop-down flap. Make sure it is the same length as the other shelves.

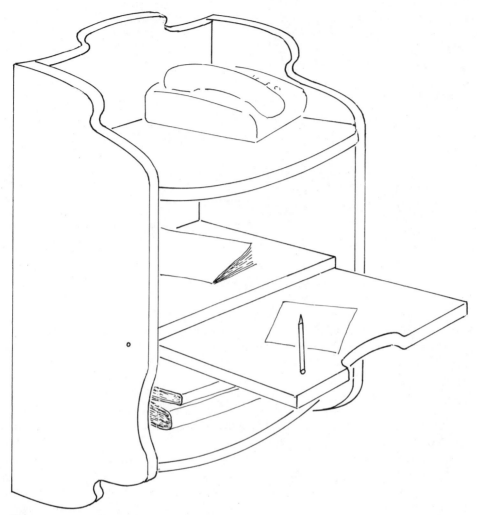

Fig. 7-10. *This telephone wall unit has a compartment which closes with a flap and a shelf for directories.*

Prepare the ends of the shelves and the sides for dowels (Fig. 7-13B).

The upper back (Fig. 7-11D and 13C) fits into the deepened rabbets, and it will be screwed from the back. Shape its top edge (Fig. 7-12C). Check that its ends will be at the same heights as the sides.

Have the plywood for the back ready, and cut sufficient dowels. Join the sides to the shelves. Glue and screw the upper back in place; then, add the plywood back to hold the assembly square. This can be held in the rabbets with glue and screws or fine nails.

The flap (Fig. 7-11E) should be an easy fit between the sides; the top edge should reach the top shelf, and the lower edge should extend 2-inches below the

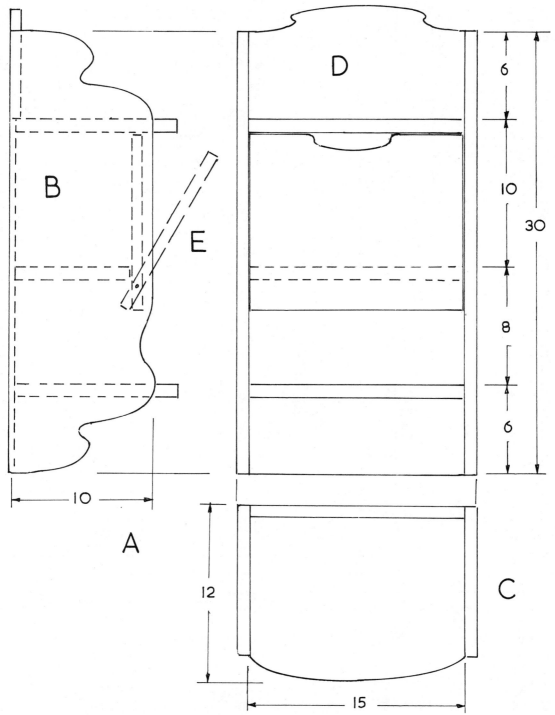

Fig. 7-11. Sizes of the telephone wall unit.

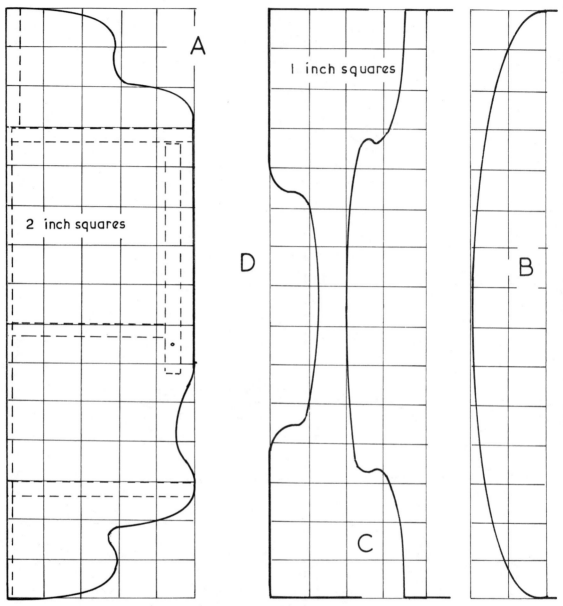

A

1 inch squares

D

2 inch squares

B

C

Fig. 7-12. Shaped parts of the telephone wall unit.

middle shelf (FIG. 7-13D). Cut away the top edge (FIG. 7-12D) to make a finger hole for moving the flap. Round the hollow to make a comfortable grip.

The flap pivots on two screws through the sides. These could be #8 gauge × 2-inch roundhead screws with washers under the heads. Drill so when the flap is lowered it is stopped under the shelf in a level position (FIG. 7-13E). Try the action

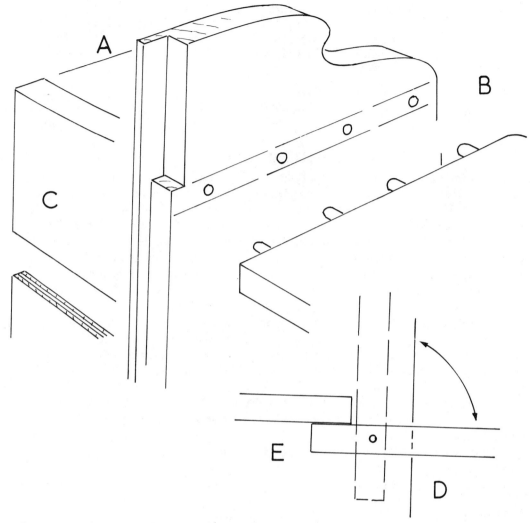

Fig. 7-13. Construction details of the telephone wall unit.

with the screws only partly driven; do not fully tighten them until the final assembly. Have close-fitting clearance holes in the sides, so the screws move with the flap.

Although the flap will be prevented from falling from the upper position by friction, you need stops under the top shelf to hold it in the closed position without it going in too far. Put a ½-inch square block in each angle under the top shelf to stop the flap when it is upright.

The finish will depend on the furniture, which has to be matched, but you will probably use stain and polish.

Materials List for Telephone Wall Unit

2 sides	¾ × 10 × 32
2 shelves	¾ × 12 × 17
1 shelf	¾ × 8½ × 17
1 flap	¾ × 12 × 17
1 back	¾ × 8 × 18
1 back	7 × 25 × ¼ plywood

BIRDS' FEEDING TABLE

If you want to watch birds while they are feeding, you will attract more if you arrange the feeding table high above the ground, where most birds feel safe. This feeding table (FIG. 7-14) has the feeding area 5 feet above the ground, so you can reach it to place food, but the birds are high enough to be away from predators. The table area is 24-inches square and a shelter is provided. Ledges around the sides will limit the amount of food which is dropped over the edges. Supports for the central post are given a bird motif, and there are many other parts which have to be shaped with a scroll saw.

Some parts are made from exterior plywood. The solid wood parts could be softwood, although they would be better made of a durable hardwood. Many parts are nailed or screwed, but dowels are needed for some parts of the brackets and waterproof glue should be used between all meeting surfaces. Besides strengthening the joints, glue will prevent the entry of water, which might cause rot.

The unit is made freestanding, so you can change its location or take it inside for storage, but you could drill the ends of the feet for spikes into the ground for additional stability.

The design (FIG. 7-15) shows a unit that is just over 6-feet high, has a table 24-inches square, and a spread of feet 30 inches. If you vary sizes, allow adequate spread at the bottom for stability. Birds tend to be messy feeders, so give them a table large enough to allow for scratching and spreading food. Things like nuts might be enclosed in fine nets or mesh under the shelter.

Start by making the platform (FIG. 7-15A). Give it a wavy outline (FIG. 7-16A). Mark the center underneath and the positions of the shelter uprights on top.

Make the four border pieces (FIG. 7-15B and 17A). Fit them with glue and screws from below (FIG. 7-16B).

Cut the shelter ends (FIG. 7-17B). Fit the uprights inside the corners (FIG. 7-17C). Make roofs (FIG. 7-17D) that will space the uprights 9-inches apart. Nail them on, and fit the end decorations (FIG. 7-16C and 17E). Check the positions of the shelter assembly on the platform. Drill for screws from below, but do not join these parts until after the platform has been mounted on the post.

The feet consist of two strips crossing with a halved joint (FIG. 7-15C).

Make a piece 6-inches across to fit on top of the feet (FIG. 7-15D). Cut a square hole in it to match the post.

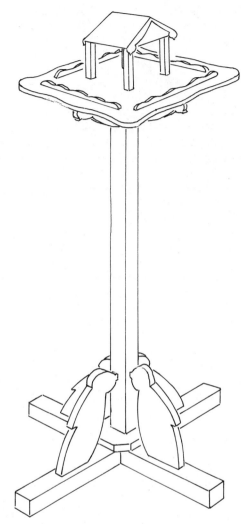

Fig. 7-14. A birds' feeding table to stand in the yard.

Cut the post to length. This should be straight-grained, and free from flaws or knots that might cause it to warp later.

Cut the four bird-shaped brackets that go under the platform (FIG. 7-16D), and the four that go between the post and the legs (FIG. 7-16E). In all cases, check that the flat surfaces are square with each other.

Prepare the brackets for ⅜-inch or ½-inch dowels into the post. Drill the post to suit.

Join the top brackets to the post with glue and dowels. Center the assembly on the inverted platform to mark locations. Drill for screws downward from the platform into the post and the brackets.

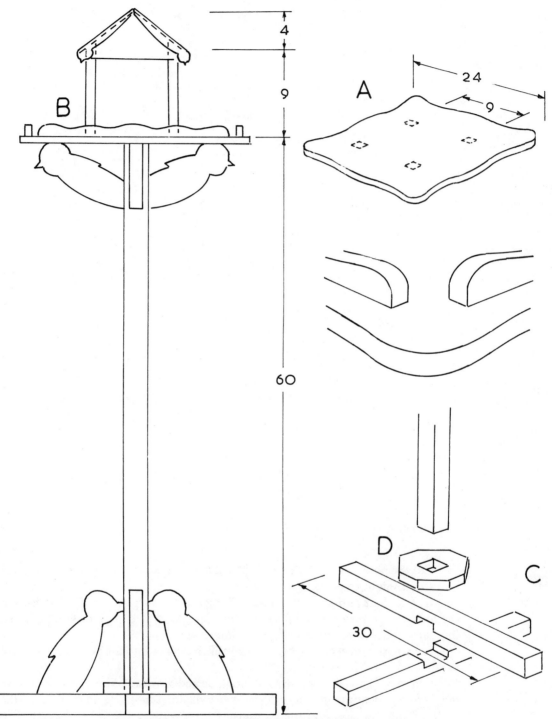

Fig. 7-15. Sizes and constructional details of the birds' feeding table.

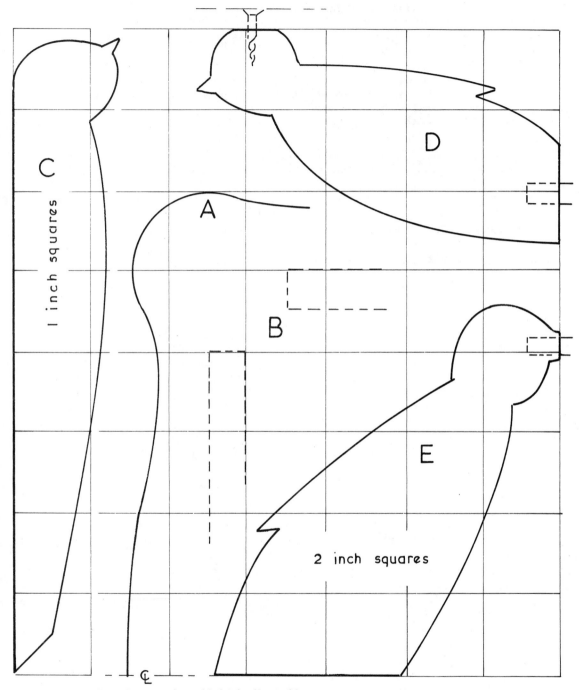

C

1 inch squares

A

B

D

E

2 inch squares

C̶L̶

Fig. 7-16. Shaped parts of the birds' feeding table.

Materials List for Birds' Feeding Table

1 platform	24 × 24 × ½ plywood
4 borders	½ × 1 × 22
4 shelter uprights	1 × 1 × 12
2 shelter ends	½ × 5 × 11
4 shelter decorations	1½ × 9 × ¼ plywood
2 feet	2 × 2 × 32
1 block	1 × 6 × 7
1 post	2 × 2 × 60
4 brackets	1 × 6 × 10
4 brackets	1 × 8 × 10

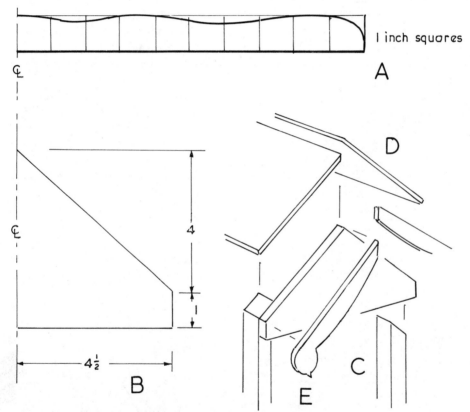

Fig. 7-17. Parts at the top of the birds' feeding table.

Screw through the platform into the uprights of the shelter.

Finish with preservative or paint. Avoid preservative on the top of the platform, as the smell may scare birds.

Deal with the bottom assembly in a similar way. To avoid having to use very long screws upwards through the feet, counterbore about halfway through to sink the screw heads. Glue the post into the block with a square hole; next, dowel the brackets to the post and screws through the feet. Check squareness in all directions while positioning the screws.

Screw the platform to the post and the four brackets, again checking squareness all ways.

TAB BOOKCASE

If you are a member of the How-to Book Club, or buy many of the TAB How-to books to help you with your hobbies and shop activities, you need somewhere to keep them where they are displayed are accessible. Nearly all TAB how-to books are in two sizes: $7\frac{1}{2}$ inches $\times 9\frac{1}{2}$ inches, and $5\frac{1}{2}$ inches $\times 8\frac{1}{2}$ inches. Of course, there are many other books close to these sizes, so if you make a bookcase to take TAB books there will be space for them as well.

Many bookcases are rather austere. They may be functional, but they are not beautiful, mainly due to their straight lines. With a scroll saw you can alter this and provide many curves to enhance the appearance of a bookcase. This bookcase has straight lines where they matter, but all other parts are curved. If you are a *how-to* enthusiast this is how to make your book storage better than the everyday mass-produced piece of furniture.

This bookcase allows for two rows of the larger TAB books and two of the smaller size, with a top shelf suitable for displaying ornaments or a pot plant (FIG. 7-18). The suggested sizes (FIG. 7-19A) bring the top row of books to eye level. You can alter the shelves, but the suggested length produces a bookcase of attractive proportions with a good capacity.

All wood is finished $\frac{5}{8}$-inch thick. The main joints are doweled. Use a furniture hardwood and stain and polish it to match surrounding furniture. Use softwood and stain and varnish it, or paint it brightly.

The sides (FIG. 7-19B) are the key parts. Mark boards to length and with the shelf positions.

Mark the reduced width of the top part, and with the shelf markings as reference points, mark the curves. The top curve loops down to the top shelf (FIG. 7-20A). The cuts between the shelves stop $1\frac{1}{2}$-inches above the lower shelf (FIG. 7-20B). Where the width of the side changes, the curve continues (FIG. 7-20C) in a loop similar to that at the top. At the bottom, cut hollows starting $2\frac{1}{2}$-inches in from back and front, and going 1-inch deep (FIG. 7-19C).

Mark the positions of the rear strips above the shelves. Mark the centers of $\frac{3}{8}$-inch dowel holes. It should be sufficient to have two dowels in each rear strip, and three in each shelf (FIG. 7-21A), but you could put four in each end of the wider shelves. The bottom shelf comes within the plinth, or base, and you could use screws through there, as the heads will be hidden by the plinth.

Cut the shelves the same length with ends carefully squared. Each shelf end should be the same width as the side, but the front edge of four shelves project

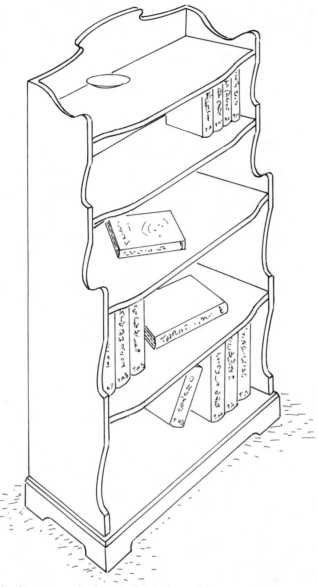

Fig. 7-18. A bookcase to suit the standard sizes of TAB publications.

forward with a shaped form (FIG. 7-20D and 21B). The front of the bottom shelf is straight across (FIG. 7-21C).

Cut all rear strips the same length as the shelves. The lower four are parallel pieces (FIG. 7-19D and 21D). Round their top edges.

The top rear strip (FIG. 7-21E) extends 3-inches above the sides; it has a shaped top (FIG. 7-20E) to complement the curves of the sides.

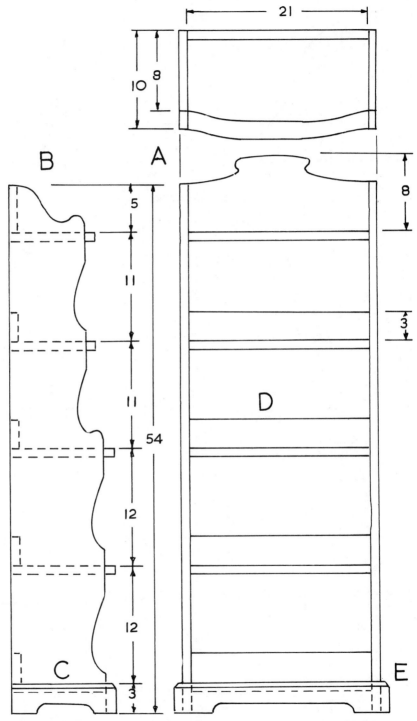

Fig. 7-19. Sizes of the bookcase.

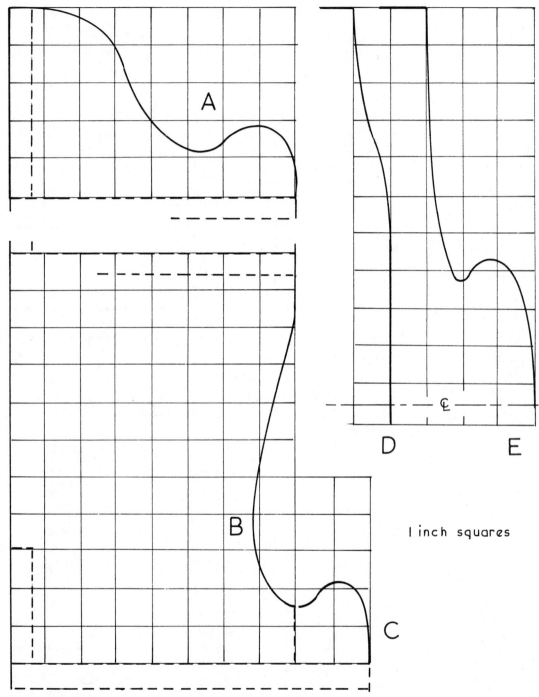

A

B

C

D **E**

℄

1 inch squares

Fig. 7-20. Shaped parts of the bookcase.

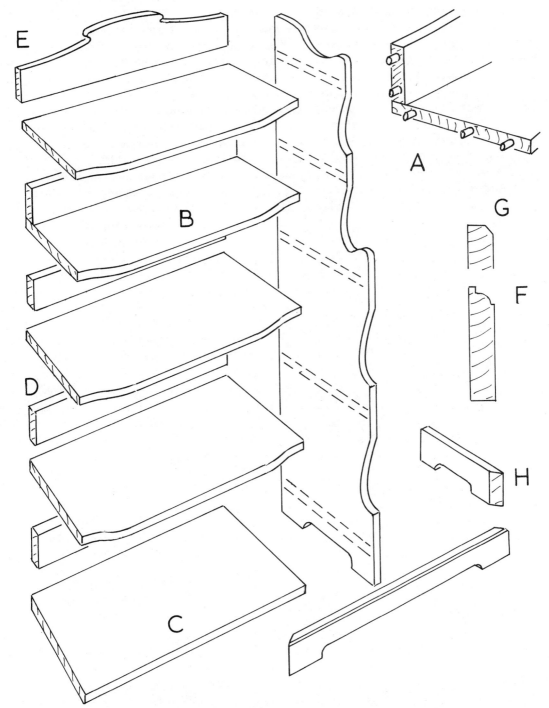

Fig. 7-21. How the parts of the bookcase fit together.

Sand all curves and take the sharpness off the edges.

Mark and drill the ends of the shelves and rear pieces to match the dowel markings on the sides. Drill the sides as deep as possible without the risk of breaking through. Drill and countersink for screws into the bottom shelf.

You could dowel rear pieces to the shelves, but as it is unlikely screw heads would show, you can glue these joints and supplement the glue with two screws driven upwards in each shelf. Join these parts before you join to the sides.

Have sufficient dowels ready; then, join all crosswise parts between the sides. Clamp tightly until the glue has set. The parts should pull square, but check that there is no twist. It is best to assemble with the back down on a flat surface.

For most situations, the plinth (FIG. 7-19E) is at the sides and front only, but if the bookcase is to stand where its back will be visible, you can carry it around the rear as well. Cut strips to the same height as the top of the bottom shelf.

If you have a suitable router cutter or other equipment, mold the top edge of the strips (FIG. 7-21F). Otherwise, a simple bevel (FIG. 7-21G) will be sufficient.

Mark and cut the plinth strips for miters at the front corners (FIG. 7-21H). Cut away the end pieces to match the shapes cut on the bookcase sides. Cut away a matching amount at the front.

You may find it sufficient to glue the plinth pieces in position. You could drive screws or nails from inside into the end pieces. The front piece may have pins into the shelf, set below the surface and the heads covered with wood fillers.

See that all meeting parts are level. Remove sharpness from edges and corners. Apply your chosen finish.

Materials List for TAB Bookcase

(All ⅝-inch thick)

2 sides	10 × 56
2 shelves	9 × 23
2 shelves	11 × 23
1 shelf	10 × 23
4 rear strips	3 × 23
1 rear strip	5 × 23
2 plinths	3 × 12
1 plinth	3 × 25

Eight

Utility Articles

There are many smaller items of use about the home and elsewhere, that are not furniture or toys, but which are of use in many ways. These utility articles are attractive to the operator of a scroll saw because they are usually of a size which can be easily manipulated through even one of the smaller machines. They give scope for interesting cuts in a comparatively small space.

If your purpose is to make things to sell in quantity, these are pieces which will find customers through craft and souvenir stores. Where parts are thin, you can cut several blocked together at one time. With care and the right blades, you can reduce the need for sanding or other finishing work on edges. Time, and therefore costs, are reduced.

These are items that should always be welcomed by family and friends, so if you are looking for something to do in your shop, which is mainly scroll saw work, these articles allow you to enjoy sawing with small pieces of wood. Know that at the end, the result will be wanted by someone.

CLOTHING HANGERS

There are plenty of metal and plastic coat hangers and similar things for looking after your clothing, but it is interesting to make your own; then you have the advantage of being able to style your products to suit your needs. These items are worthwhile scroll saw projects and they will use up odd pieces of plywood and hardwood. This gives you yet another opportunity to stamp your individuality on the things you use, instead of just being dependent on mass-produced products.

Coat hangers are best made of hardwood plywood, about ⅜-inch (9mm) thick. It might be thinner for light use, but if you choose softwood plywood it will have to be thicker, which will not matter. Rounding edges is advisable, and thorough rounding of thicker plywood will lighten its appearance.

It is the hooks in the hangers where the strength of hardwood plywood is needed, as cross-sections have to be as slight as possible to avoid a clumsy appearance.

If you intend making several coat hangers of the same type, cut one first and use it as a template before doing any rounding of edges. If you will be making a variety, it may be worthwhile making a hardboard or thin plywood template of the hook, which can be the same for most hangers.

The basic hanger is a simple bow (FIG. 8-1A). Check the length which would be best for your suits or coats. The example is 16-inches across.

You may find more uses for a similar hanger with a bar across to take slacks (FIG. 8-1B). Avoid anything angular in the outlines and round all edges; then give a final sanding.

For ladies' clothing with loops or shoulder straps, you can include a hook at each end (FIG. 8-2A) without spoiling the hanger for coats or other clothing that will go over the top. Extend any hanger with extra rails below (FIG. 8-2B), so you can accommodate three or more pairs of slacks or other items that will wrap over rails.

If you only need to hang slacks, make a hanger that is not much more than a slotted piece (FIG. 8-2C).

Neckties might be hung over the rail of a coat rack, but it would be neater and more convenient to give them their own rack. The tie racks suggested here are intended to hang from hooks or nails, so they can be taken down when you want to select or hang a necktie or belt. Close-grained hardwood could be used, but these racks are particularly suitable for cutting in hardwood plywood about ¼-inch (6mm) thick, and would then make good selling items, if that is your intention.

A simple rack consists of a series of slots (FIG. 8-3A). It could be made any length, although for a large number of neckties or belts it might be better to arrange two rows of slots or make two racks. Take the sharpness off all edges, including the insides of the slots, but there is no need for much rounding of this or the following racks.

There is an advantage in being able to put ties on or off a rack from the sides, so you could make one with open arms (FIG. 8-3B). The arm heights are staggered to give strength to the central upright part. If you want to make the arms on opposite sides at the same levels, the central part should be widened. Like the first design, you could make this rack to any length.

The other design (FIG. 8-4) combines slots and open arms. To keep level it has to be hung from two hooks. The word *ties* makes the use obvious and may be an attraction if you make to sell. If it would be appropriate, you could alter the name to *belts*. If you use solid wood, arrange the grain across the rack. The nibs in the slots will separate ties, but if you want to pack in more ties the slot edges could be cut straight.

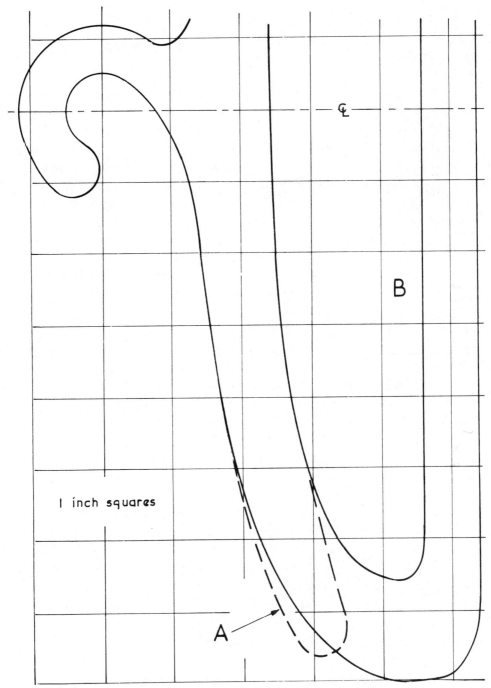

C̶L

B

1 inch squares

A

Fig. 8-1. The basic shape of a coat hanger.

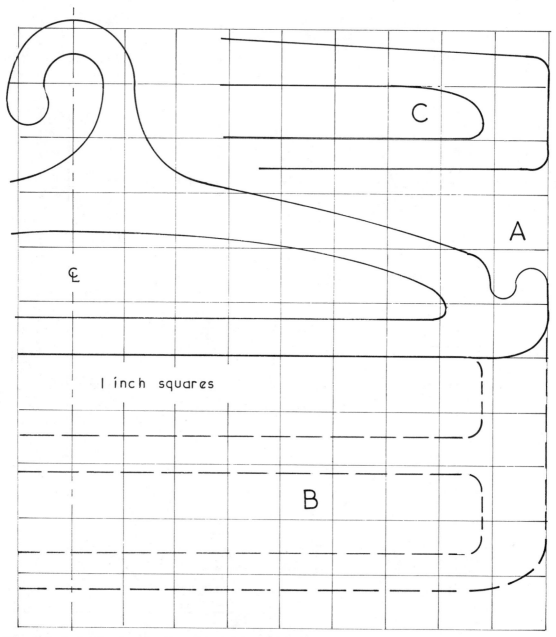

1 inch squares

Fig. 8-2. A clothing hanger that might be extended.

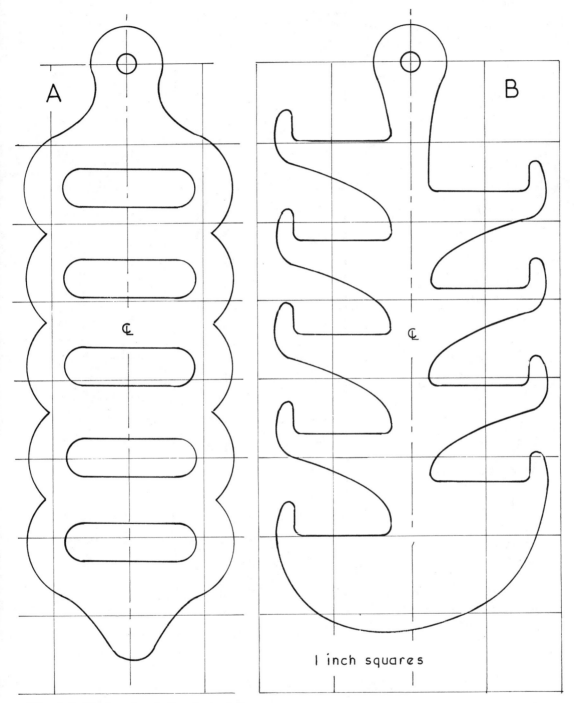

Fig. 8-3. *Shapes of racks for ties or belts.*

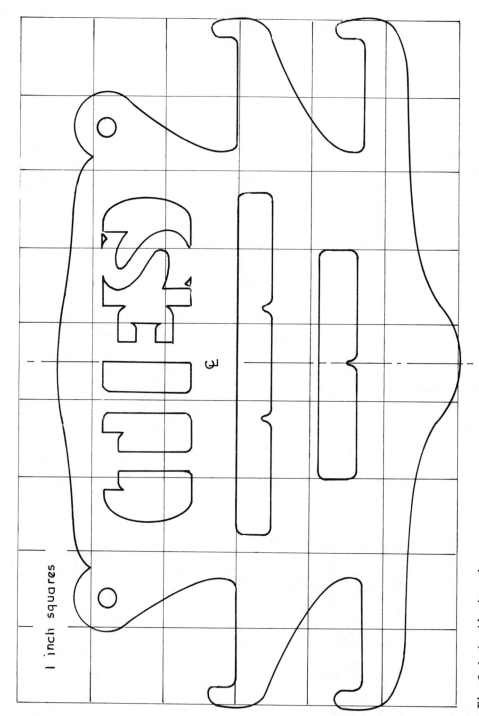

1 inch squares

Fig. 8-4. A wide tie rack.

KITCHEN TOOLS

Many expert cooks prefer kitchen tools made from wood to those made from plastic or metal. It is possible to make any of these tools with a scroll saw. You will be able to produce tools to suit your requirements and in a variety to cope with differing food preparation needs, instead of having to accept bought tools which may not be just right for you.

Wood for use in connection with food always has to be selected for its hygienic properties. Avoid resinous or oily woods. Choose close grain. Avoid the openness seen in such woods as oak. Close grain usually means few prominent markings. Color may not affect hygiene, but a light color looks cleaner. Sycamore for example, has a light color, close grain and even appearance, but there are many others. The tools (Fig. 8-5) do not require very big pieces of wood; you should be able to pick wood without knots or other flaws. Planing a surface will show if the wood is flawless.

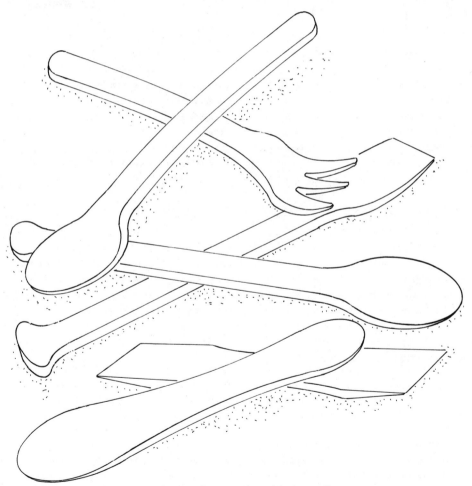

Fig. 8-5. A selection of kitchen tools to make with a scroll saw.

A good stirrer (FIG. 8-6A) looks like a spade, but is intended for mixing, particularly when the ingredients may form a rather stiff mass. The widened handle allows for twisting without difficulty. For some mixing there is an advantage in having three or more holes through the blade (FIG. 8-6B). Thin the end, which may be square across or angled, to a rounded edge; well round the parts that will be handled.

A tool with a rounded end and a narrower handle (FIG. 8-6C) may be preferred for stirring thinner ingredients. It may also be used as a spoon. Thin its end and round the handle in the same way as the first stirrer.

A spatula is a tool for more delicate work. It may be used for mixing, but it can also shape pastry or arrange cake decorations. One with rounded ends (FIG. 8-6D) has its ends tapered almost to knife edges for scraping and cutting. The tapering is shown one-sided (FIG. 8-6E). An alternative is to provide straight ends (FIG. 8-6F) for angular cutting and scraping. An advantage of cutting your own kitchen tools is that you do not have to follow tradition, and you can make stirrers and spatulas of any shape (FIG. 8-6G).

Salad servers are made in pairs. Flat ones should be satisfactory, but they are much better shaped, although this involves curves both ways (FIG. 8-7A and B). How much shaping you can give depends on the capacity of your machine. The suggested patterns are intended to be cut from 2-inch square wood. You could make the spoon and fork slightly smaller if your scroll saw will only cut thinner wood, but salad servers are better if kept fairly large. The spoon and fork are made in the same way, except for the different ends.

Mark out the shapes on two faces of the wood (FIG. 8-7C). Note that the side view should be thickest at the top of the curve (FIG. 8-7D) to provide strength where the grain is shorter. Cut the outline one way; then tape the parts together again ready to cut the other way.

In the fork end, it is advisable to drill holes (about $3/16$ inch) at the tops of the cuts (FIG. 8-7E) before sawing. This reduces any risk of later splitting.

Clean off all saw marks and round the edges by sanding.

Wooden kitchen tools may be left untreated, but there is then a risk of water absorption due to frequent washing; this may lead to cracks or distortion. You can limit this by soaking the tools in vegetable cooking oil. Soak for an hour; then wipe off. Do this again at intervals when more protection seems necessary.

Materials List for Kitchen Tools

Stirrer	$3/8 \times$	2×25
Spatula	$5/16 \times 1^{1/2} \times 11$	
Salad servers	$2 \times$	2×15

CLOCK STANDS

Clocks and other instruments with dials, such as barometers and thermometers, are very suitable for mounting in decorated wooden stands or frames. The dial is round and its surrounding rim or bezel is usually round, so mounting the

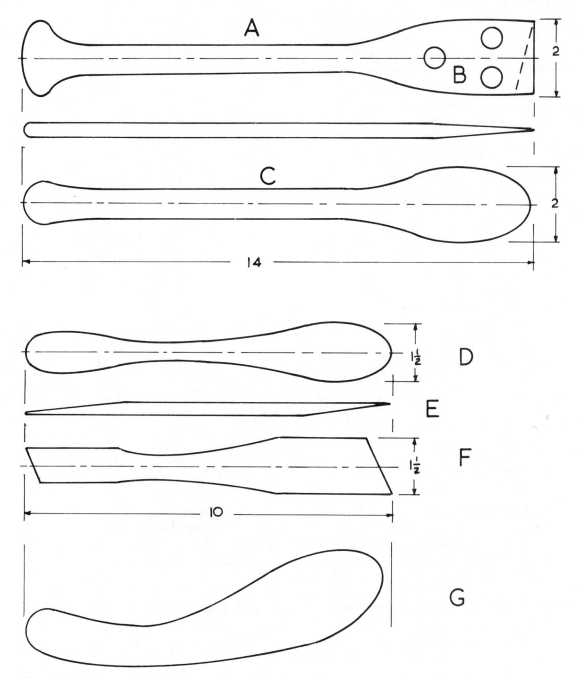

Fig. 8-6. Outlines of flat kitchen tools.

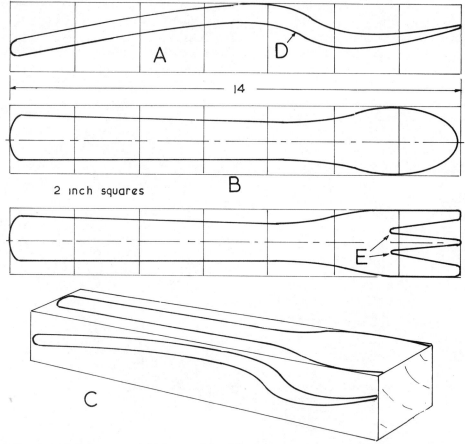

A

D

|← —————————————— 14 —————————————— →|

2 inch squares

B

E

C

Fig. 8-7. Salad servers which are shaped both ways.

clock movement through a hole gives you scope for a decorative wooden form, ranging from a comparatively simple outline which puts the emphasis on the dial, to an elaborately fretted piece of work in which the dial is only a small part. Some examples are suggested here; you can adapt many other designs to accommodate a clock or other instrument mounted on a base.

Clock and other instrument sizes vary considerably in the front diameter, which is the controlling dimension for planning your design. Some have a round body not much smaller, while others have comparatively small works behind the dial. The method of fitting varies, and you will have to arrange what is cut out to bring the dial central while allowing space for the movement and the securing arrangement. In many cases, you can make a round hole as the woodwork may not have to be a close fit on the projections behind the face.

The basic clock stand consists of an upright piece to hold the clock or other instrument mounted on a flat base. With a scroll saw, you can include plenty of shaping of both parts.

The first pattern (FIG. 8-8) is designed around a clock with an outside diameter of 4 inches and with a round body that passes through the wood (FIG. 8-9A). However, the same outlines could be used for a clock with a dial between 3 inches and 5 inches, with the cutout arranged to suit the particular movement.

This stand is intended to be made of ⅝-inch hardwood. Mark out the upright part (FIG. 8-9B) with a cutout to suit the clock. The grain should go across the wood. The outline is most effective if left squarely from a clean cut, with just the sharpness taken off the edges.

Mark and cut the base (FIG. 8-9C) in the same way. Mark the position of the other part and drill for three screws. Countersink so the heads will pull below the bottom surface. Assemble with a little glue, or rely only on the screws. Cloth glued to the bottom of the base will prevent slipping or marking a polished surface. Finish to suit surroundings and the clock face. Most clock dials are a light color, and they look best on stained wood finished with a moderate gloss.

An alternative way of joining the parts of a clock stand is to have the base the same length as the upright piece and groove it (FIG. 8-9D). If this is made a close fit, you should not need screws as much as glue.

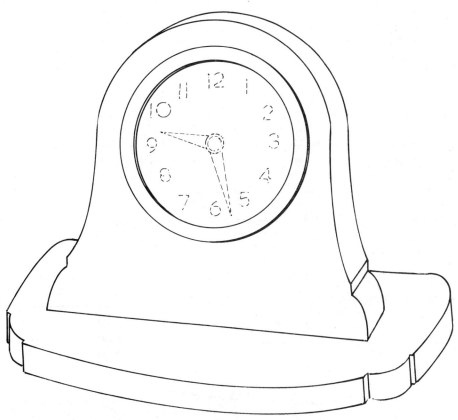

Fig. 8-8. A stand on a base to hold a clock.

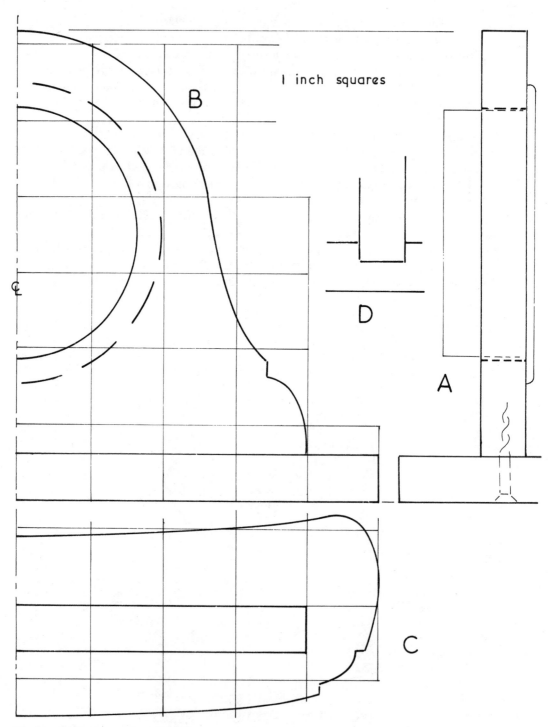

1 inch squares

B

C̵

D

A

C

Fig. 8-9. The parts of a clock stand.

If a clock or other instrument is to be at eye level, it is appropriate to arrange it upright. If it is to be lower, as on a table, it would be better tilted back slightly. Besides making viewing easier, it will enhance the appearance.

In most cases the tilt should be slight. Try tilting a piece of wood to determine the best angle, but this will probably be about 80 degrees to the table. For stability you will have to extend the base further at the back. The weight of the clock should be at about the center of the width of the base (FIG. 8-10A).

For a small stand it might be strong enough to only screw through the base, but for any stand it helps in appearance as well as strength to include a pair of small brackets (FIG. 8-10B) arranged on each side of the clock back. It should be sufficient to glue them in place. They need not be as thick as the upright part.

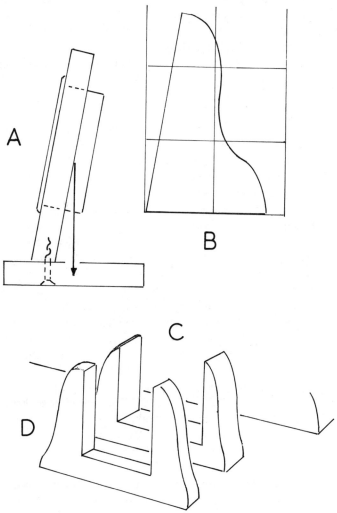

Fig. 8-10. The clock can be arranged to tilt.

Of the various instruments you may wish to mount, barometer dials tend to be bigger than clocks and thermometer dials are smaller. If you wish to mount a thermometer and a barometer together on a stand, the vertical part of the stand must allow for this. For a hanging arrangement, you could put the smaller thermometer above the barometer, but on a stand they may be side-by-side. The same would apply to a clock and thermometer. A possible arrangement is shown (FIG. 8-11A). A barometer dial is much bigger than the hole that has to be cut out. When laying out your instrument positions, arrange the lower edges of the rims to come level (FIG. 8-11B). Then cut out to suit.

The pattern shown is intended to be cut from wood ⅝-inch or ¾-inch thick. The base could be similar to that for the first design (FIG. 8-9C), and may have the instruments upright or tilted.

You can personalize a clock stand; this is particularly suitable for a presentation instrument. Initials may be added as an overlay on the stand (FIG. 8-11C). Choose wood for the initials overlay no more than 3/16-inch thick, in a contrasting color to the ⅝-inch upright. The design is shown for a clock 3-inches across the rim. You may have to alter the outline for a different size; this also applies to accommodating the initials. You could use a badge instead of initials, or arrange stylized flowers or other symbols.

You could cut separate initials, but a slight overlap allows the overlay to be a single piece. Lay out and cut the initials first. Set out the upright and mark it to match the top of the overlay (FIG. 8-11D).

Cut the upright part to shape with a hole to suit the clock. If this or the overlay is to be stained to provide a contrast, do this before gluing on the overlay. Check that the extending edges match.

Mount the upright on a base similar to that for the first design (FIG. 8-9C). Apply a finish with a moderate gloss.

Combine a clock with a calendar. It could be a pad which you glue on and replace each year, but it would be better to provide a socket for the separate lettered and numbered plastic pieces that show each day (FIG. 8-12). The clock could be any size, but the design is intended for one about 4-inches across the rim (FIG. 8-13A). You will need to get the plastic date pieces before starting work, to measure their overall sizes and the thickness needed to hold the pack.

Lay out the shape to include a suitable cutout for the clock and the holder for the calendar. Allow for space around and above the calendar pieces.

The calendar holder consists of a rear trough, or container, to hold the pieces (FIG. 8-10C) and a front frame which overlaps the trough by about ⅛ inch (FIG. 8-10D) to retain the pieces. Make the trough thick enough to hold all calendar pieces with a little to spare. You have to be able to put the pieces in and out easily, but do not have excess clearance. While cutting these parts you will have weak cross grain at some places, so care is needed, but when the holder is glued in place there will be enough combined strength. Cut the pieces with the grain square to each other, plywood fashion, for extra strength. Glue these pieces together and trim the outsides to match. Make sure there is no excess glue inside to interfere with fitting the calendar pieces.

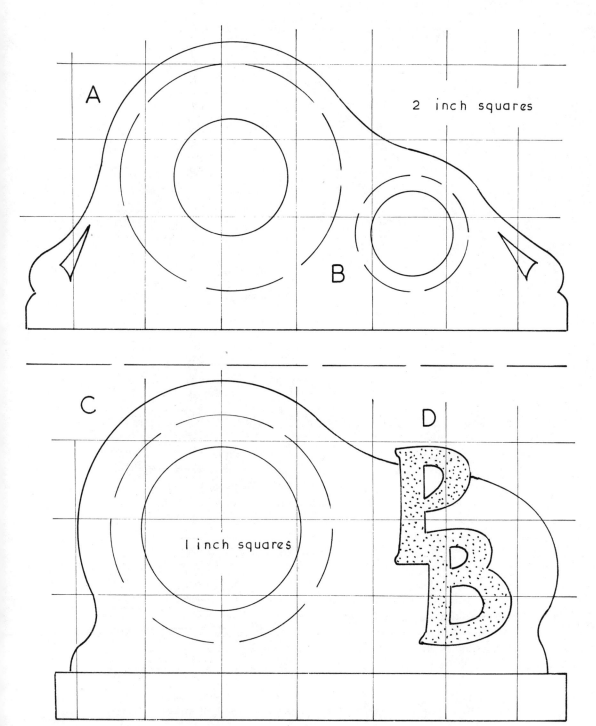

A

2 inch squares

B

C

1 inch squares

D

B

Fig. 8-11. A stand can be extended to hold instruments or a decoration at one side.

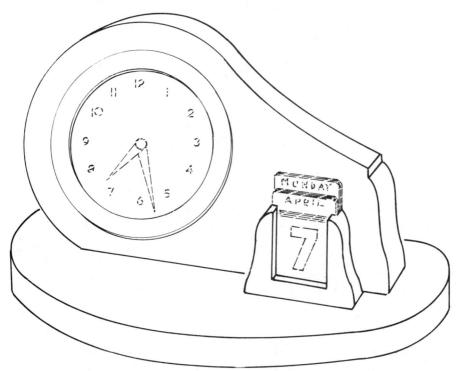

Fig. 8-12. This clock stand can also hold a calendar.

Cut the upright part to shape (FIG. 8-13B). Note that the shape at one end should be similar to that on a calendar support side.

You could make a base with straight sides, but the example shown (FIG. 8-13C) is fully curved. Mark the position of the upright and drill for three screws. Glue and screw these parts; then, add the calendar holder tight into the angle. Finish with stain and polish. A dark color will make a good background to both clock and calendar.

A clock may be mounted on a pair of pedestals, so you can tilt it to any angle you wish. This clock (FIG. 8-14) is designed for a dial 4-inches across the rim, but it is adaptable to other sizes. The clock is set in a $5/8$-inch piece of wood (FIG. 8-15A), and it has screws through two $1/2$-inch pedestals (FIG. 8-15B), which are tenoned into a base (FIG. 8-15C). The stand looks best if made of an attractive hardwood. Roundhead screws through washers should be brass or plated.

Mark out the wood for the clock, and make a hole to suit the movement. Have the grain across and make sure the opposite sides are straight and parallel. Mark screw positions on the straight edges opposite the center of the clock. Cut the outline and the holes.

Mark out and cut the pair of pedestals, with clearance holes for the screws and tenons at the bottom. Take the sharpness off the three pieces, but otherwise leave the edges square.

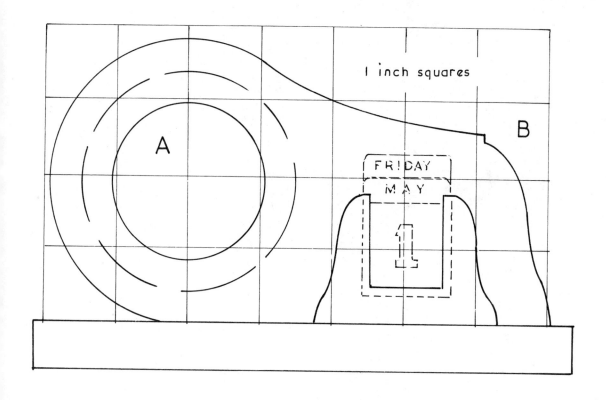

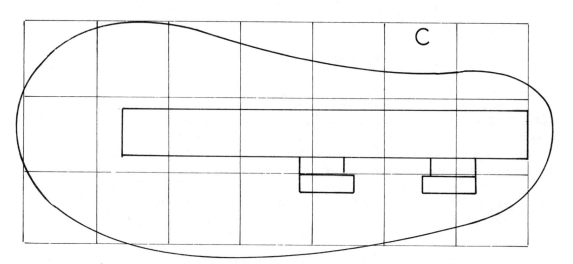

Fig. 8-13. Sizes for a stand with a clock and calendar.

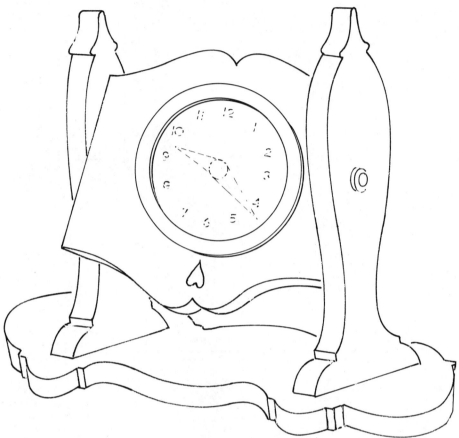

Fig. 8-14. This stand permits the angle of the clock to be altered.

When you mark out the base, (FIG. 8-16A) work about centerlines and check that the distance between mortises matches the length of the piece that takes the clock; otherwise, the parts will not assemble squarely.

Cut the base to size, and make the mortises to match the tenons (FIG. 8-16B). It will not matter if the tenons are too long at this stage because they can be leveled after fitting.

Glue the tenons into the mortises. Check squareness and use the clock piece to test spacing. Make a temporary assembly and check swinging action. If this is satisfactory, you might wish to withdraw the screws so you can finish the parts before final assembly. You could treat all parts the same, but darkening the piece with the clock makes an attractive contrast.

FRETWORK PHOTOGRAPH FRAMES

Articles with a multiplicity of fine holes cut to shape provide plenty of scope for exercising your skill with a scroll saw. There is a considerable amount of careful

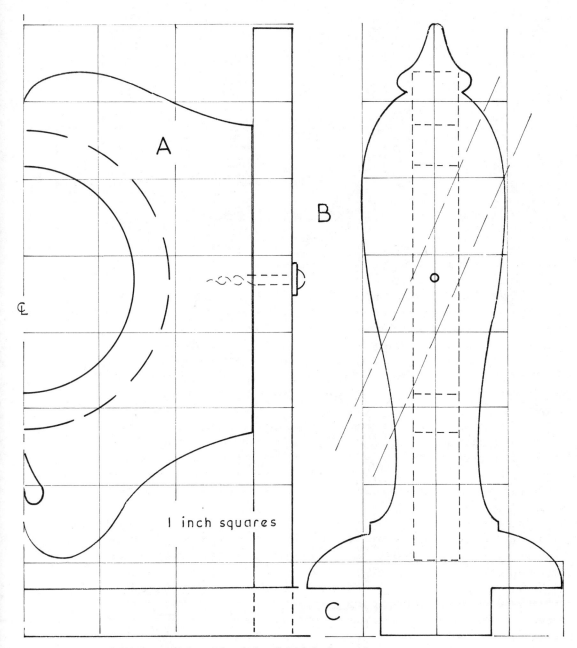

A

B

℄

1 inch squares

C

O

Fig. 8-15. Sizes of the upright parts of the tilting clock stand.

work which you will not want to waste, so it is advisable to start with a good piece of wood, that is not only of fine appearance, but is free from flaws that might result in breakages later, especially in cross-grained features in the design. Attractive grain marking may be worth having, but that may indicate differences in

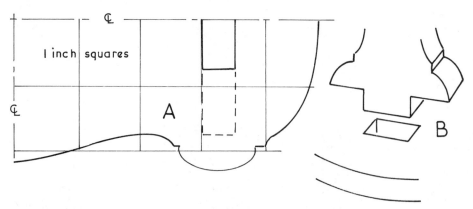

Fig. 8-16. The shape of the base and joint details for the tilting clock stand.

strength in the wood. It is the cutting out which forms the decoration, so a plain strong close-grained wood makes a good choice.

Start with wood of an even thickness and with good surfaces. The design is best drawn on paper with a pattern of squares enlarged from the original drawing. Attach the paper to the wood with an adhesive that will hold it there during cutting, but which will allow the paper to be pealed away when all cuts have been made. A water-soluble adhesive will allow you to soak off the paper.

Picture frames are suitable subjects for fretted designs. Those described here may be cut from solid wood or hardwood plywood up to $\frac{3}{8}$-inch thick, with $\frac{1}{4}$-inch overlays.

The first photograph frame (FIG. 8-17) is drawn on 1-inch squares and is suitable for a photograph 6 inches × 8 inches. Vary the size by using a grid of squares of a different size. The photograph fits the opening, and there is an overlay covering it with an overlay of $\frac{3}{16}$-inch all round (FIG. 8-17A). Prepare your drawing of the main part symmetrical about its centerline, and cut it out (FIG. 8-17B).

When you cut the overlay (FIG. 8-17C) there will be some short grain that will need careful handling, but that will be held safely when it is glued to the frame. Take care with the straight inner edges; any discrepancies will be very apparent in the finished frame. Glue the overlay in place.

Make the strut (FIG. 8-17D) of a length that will allow a hinge to be fitted immediately above the photograph opening, when the strut is folded with its bottom edge level with the bottom of the frame. Use a light brass hinge about $1\frac{1}{2}$-inches long.

One way of holding the photograph and glass is to back these with cardboard, and use a few pins around the edges (FIG. 8-17E).

The second frame (FIG. 8-18) is drawn to suit a photograph or picture 8 inches × 10 inches, but you could adapt it to suit other sizes by altering the size of the grid

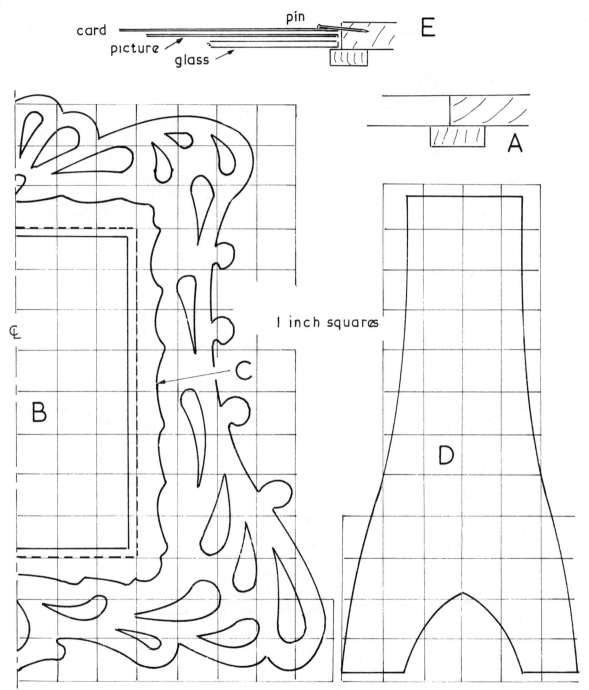

card

picture

glass

pin

E

A

1 inch squares

B

C

D

Fig. 8-17. Pattern for a standing fretwork photograph frame.

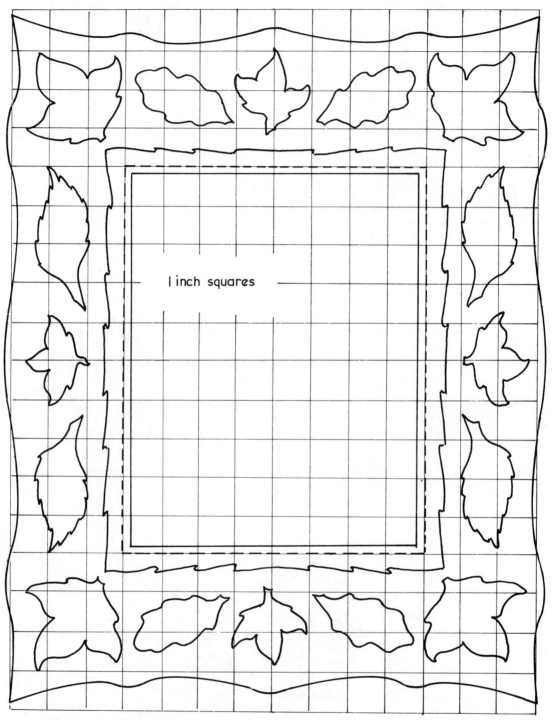

1 inch squares

Fig. 8-18. Pattern for a hanging fretwork photograph frame.

squares. With its leaf motif, it is particularly suitable for framing a rural scene. The frame is intended to hang either way up, but it could be given a strut similar to the first design if you want it to stand.

You could cut the frame from solid wood, but because of its size you may prefer a hardwood plywood ⅜-inch thick. The overlay could be ¼-inch solid wood of a contrasting color. The design is symmetrical, so when preparing your pattern you could draw half the design and print a copy for the other half.

Mount the picture and glass in the same way as suggested for the first frame. A piece of Formica or other flat thin plastic would hold the picture flatter than cardboard.

The third frame (FIG. 8-19) takes advantage of the versatility of a scroll saw in making accurate sloping cuts. The four decorative shapes are made with angular cuts, so they can be pushed forward to look like overlays (FIG. 8-19A).

The frame is drawn to suit a picture 4 inches × 5 inches. Instead of an overlay on the front to retain it, it fits inside a frame on the back (FIG. 8-19B and C), so it appears through a shaped cutout in the main part of the frame.

All parts are ⅜-inch thick. Use hardwood plywood for the rear frame and the strut, but the front will look best in an attractive hardwood.

Mark out all details of the main frame, and cut the outline with square edges. Experiment with scrap wood with the blade to be used, so the tilt will allow the decorative pieces to push forward about ⅛ inch (FIG. 8-19D).

The picture opening could be cut with square edges, or you might tilt the saw (FIG. 8-19E). If you have a suitable router cutter, the edges might be rounded (FIG. 8-19F).

Secure the pushed-out pieces with glue. Check that they are all at the same level.

The rear frame has straight edges and is ½-inch wide all round. Match its size to the picture. Glue it in place.

Make the strut (FIG. 8-19G) to reach from the top of the rear frame to the bottom edge of the front part when folded. Hinge it to the rear frame. Secure the picture and glass in the same way as suggested for the other two frames.

PLASTIC ITEMS

Although most things made with a scroll saw will be cut from wood, you can cut plastic and metal with suitable blades, so you can make things entirely from these materials or combine them with wood. The plastics most suitable are the hard sheet materials, such as Plexiglass, for which there are adhesives which soften the surfaces to give a weld-like joint, so many items can be made without screws or cut joints.

A benefit of Plexiglass and plastics of its type is the high gloss already on the surface, protected by paper which can be peeled off after cutting; this also gives you a good surface on which to draw your pattern. Edges may have a matt finish, as left by the saw, or they can be polished. Polished Plexiglass has a clarity greater than glass, so a fully polished piece has a crystal look. Of course, it is not as hard as glass, so surfaces will eventually deteriorate.

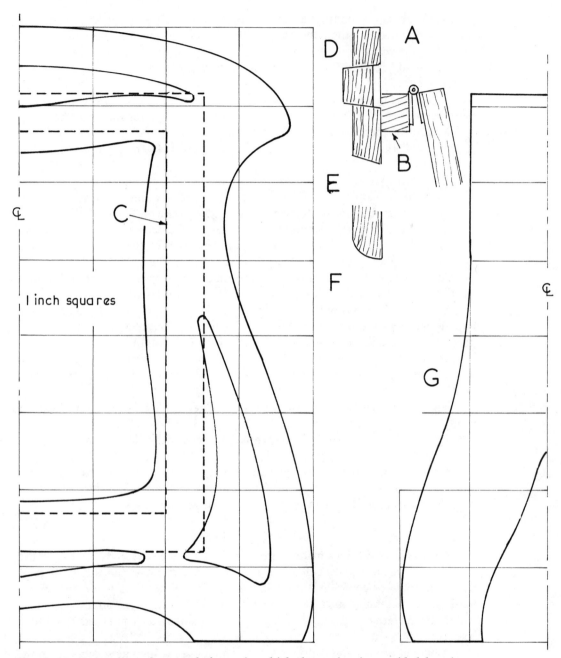

1 inch squares

Fig. 8-19. A standing photograph frame in which decoration is provided by pieces raised from the background.

Some articles intended for light wood construction may also be made from sheet plastic, or you could combine the two. A plastic lid or handle may go on a wood box. The cutout animals described earlier would look good in colored plastic on wood bases.

The patterns included in this project are intended to be cut mainly from plastic.

Dog Photograph Stand

This stand (FIG. 8-20A) is drawn to suit a photograph trimmed to 3½ inches × 5½ inches. The photograph is held by two pieces of ⅛-inch clear plastic, or one piece and a piece of thick cardboard. The supporting dogs have red or black

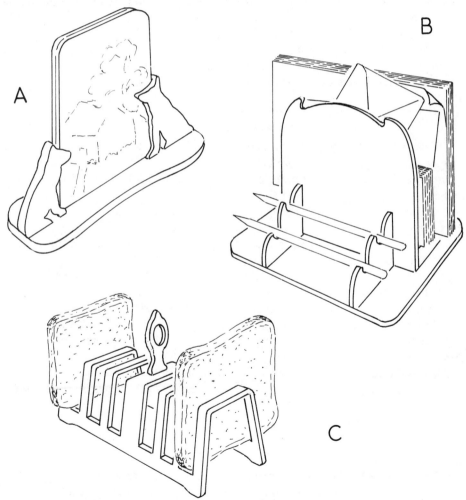

Fig. 8-20. Three items made from plastic with a scroll saw.

outside pieces, with clear or colored blocks between. The base may be clear or colored.

If you alter the design, arrange for the outside animal pieces to support the photograph and its covers at two levels—in this case, between the paws as well as the heads.

Mark out the outside dog shapes (Fig. 8-21A and B), and cut two thicknesses of each at the same time.

From one each of these pieces, mark the center parts cut back to straight lines (Fig. 8-21C and D). The center pieces may have tenons (Fig. 8-21E) to go through the base.

Stick these parts together. Clean off any excess glue. Sand and polish the edges.

Cut the base to shape (Fig. 8-21F). When you cut the slots for the tenons, check that the width between the upright parts of the dog assemblies will suit the width of the photograph.

Stick the supports to the base.

Cut the transparent front (Fig. 8-21G) for the photograph. If there is sufficient space, cut a second one. You might be able to have photographs back-to-back. Otherwise, cut a piece of stiff cardboard to go behind the photograph.

Pen and Paper Stand

This item is a stand for two pens or pencils, and letters, envelopes and a supply of notepaper (Fig. 8-20B). The sizes suggested (Fig. 8-22) will take any normal pens, and a large number of sheets of paper up to about 7 inches × 9 inches.

All parts may be ⅛-inch Plexiglass, with a ¾-inch × 1-inch wood spacer. Use transparent or translucent plastic throughout or mix colors.

Cut the back (Fig. 8-22A) and front (Fig. 8-22B) to shape. See that the widths match and they are square to the base.

The wood spacer (Fig. 8-22C) is best made of hardwood. It could be stained or painted to match the plastic.

Drill the plastic for woodscrews, and join these parts to the wood. Three roundhead brass #4 gauge × ½ inch should be satisfactory in each piece.

Cut the two pen stands (Fig. 8-22D), preferably the double thickness at the same time, so they match.

Make the base (Fig. 8-22E) 4½ inches × 8 inches, with rounded corners.

Mount the paper holder with two or three countersunk screws up through the base.

Stick the pen racks in place.

TOAST RACK

This is a rack for six pieces of toast (Fig. 8-20C), with a central ring handle. It is made from ⅛-inch Plexiglass or similar plastic (Fig. 8-23). Construction involves bending over a simple former.

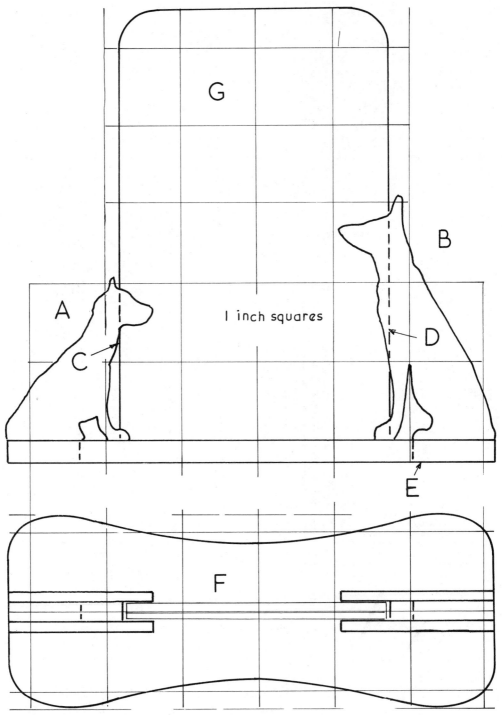

Fig. 8-21. The dog supports hold a picture and its covers.

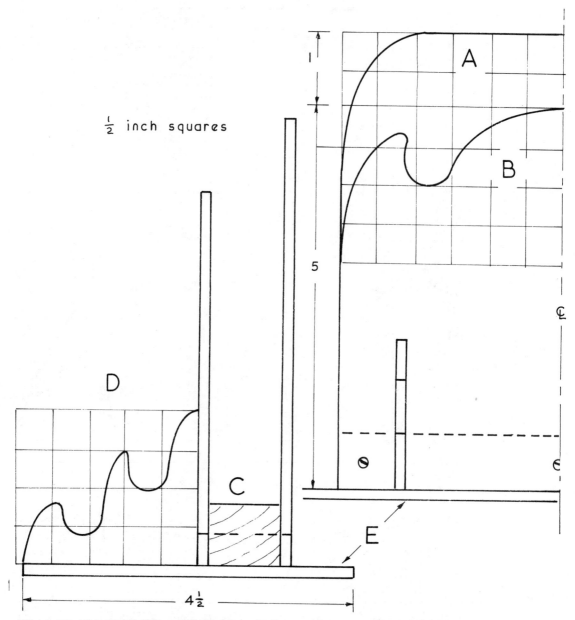

½ inch squares

A

B

C

D

C

E

1

5

4½

Fig. 8-22. This rack holds pencils on shaped pieces and papers and envelopes at the back.

Some pieces of plastic will soften enough to bend after soaking for a period in boiling water, but others need the greater heat of a domestic oven. If you are unsure of which type you have, try a scrap piece first for a few minutes in boiling water. If this procedure does not work try for a short period in a warm oven. This will show you how much time to allow for the toast rack plastic.

You could make the rack of transparent or colored plastic; the handle need not be the same color as the main rack.

Mark out the main part (FIG. 8-23A). Cut the openings and the outline. The edges are slightly hollowed, so the finished rack will stand on small corner feet. If necessary, true the straight edges of the cutouts with abrasive paper wrapped around a flat piece of wood.

Make the handle (FIG. 8-23B and C). Cut a tenon on the bottom, and make a mortise to suit it at the center of the main part (FIG. 8-23D). This should be an easy fit to allow space for adhesive. If the tenon projects slightly, the joint will be stronger.

The edges of the handle should be polished, even if you leave the edges of the other parts matt.

Prepare the wood block former (FIG. 8-23E). It should be a little longer than the rack, and tapered to match the intended shape of the toast rack. Round the upper edges. Cover the former with soft cloth laid smoothly. It could be wrapped underneath and glued or stapled there, but do not strain it.

Wear gloves, and have a piece of soft cloth ready. Soften the plastic. It will probably become very limp. Drape it over the former and check that all bars are straight before it hardens. Some light hand pressure should be enough to get the rack into shape. Allow it to cool completely.

Attach the handle with adhesive. Wash the rack with detergent and warm water. In further washing, it should not be affected by normal hand washing, as heat has to penetrate before it will soften again.

TABLE SERVERS

Show your skill with the scroll saw by making a pair of holders for jars and bottles often needed at meal time (FIG. 8-24). One holder is for two pots or jars of food like jelly, which has to be spooned out. The two spoons hang on the central handle. The other holder is similar, but it holds two bottles of sauce or dressing.

You might have to adjust sizes to suit your needs, but the sizes given (FIGS. 8-25 and 27) suit pots or jars 2½ inches in diameter and up to 5-inches high, with holders for two spoons of average size, as well as two bottles up to 2½ inches in diameter and more than 6-inches high. The drawings and instructions apply to these sizes; you will have to change some dimensions if your contents are very different.

The parts are best made of an attractive hardwood, which is given a clear finish. Boat varnish is a good finish to withstand moisture. You could use plywood, but it should be hardwood; then you can finish it with paint. If you use different finished thicknesses from those in the materials list, joint sizes will have

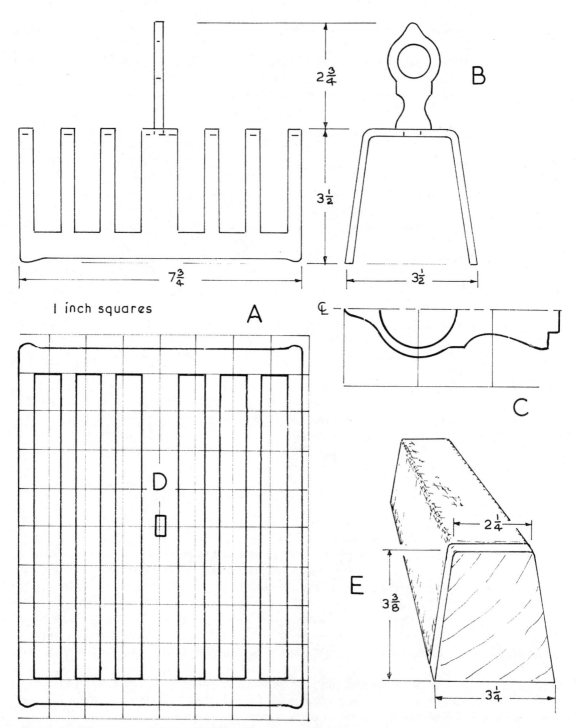

I inch squares

A

B

C

D

E

$2\frac{3}{4}$

$3\frac{1}{2}$

$3\frac{1}{2}$

$7\frac{3}{4}$

$2\frac{1}{4}$

$3\frac{3}{8}$

$3\frac{1}{4}$

Fig. 8-23. The toast rack is made by bending the cut sheet over a former.

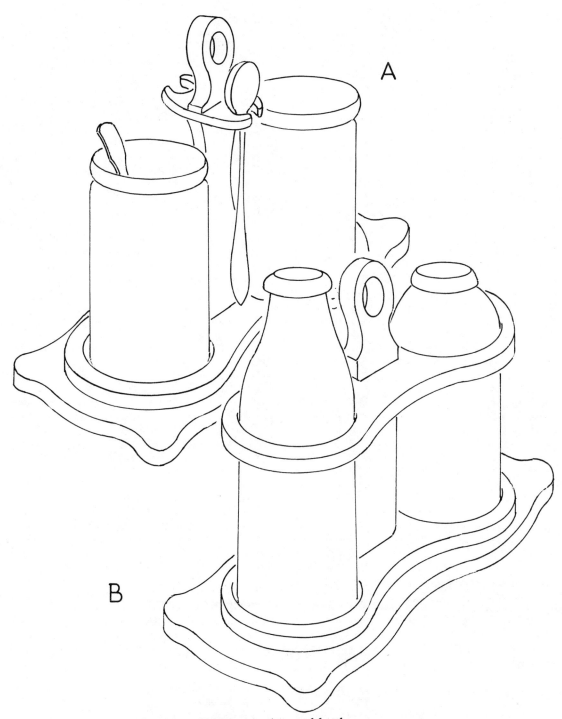

Fig. 8-24. Two table servers to hold pots or jars and bottles.

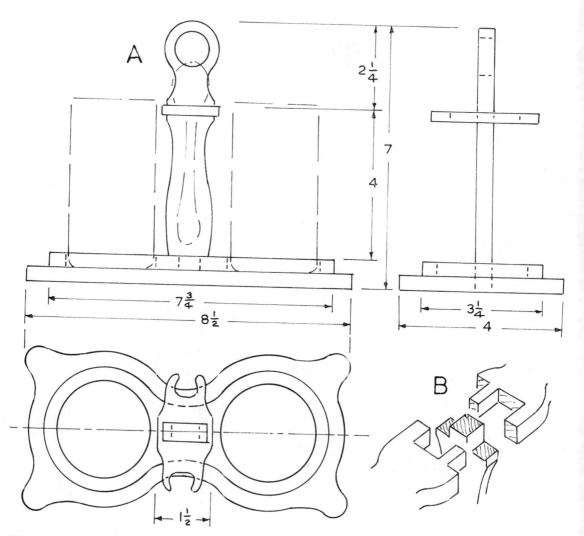

Fig. 8-25. *The pot stand also holds two spoons.*

to be altered. The pot and spoon stand is described first; then the bottle stand has several parts made in the same way. If you intend making both items you can cut some pieces, such as the base parts, for both things at the same time by stacking them to cut the shape.

Mark out the two parts of the base of the pot and spoon stand first (FIG. 8-24A). The top piece (FIG. 8-26A) has holes for the pots. The bottom piece (FIG. 8-26B) is solid, except for the mortise, which goes through both pieces. You may wish to leave cutting the mortise until you can match the tenon to it.

The finger hole in the handle (FIG. 8-25A and 26C) could be drilled before you cut the outline, when the risk of splitting is minimal. Alternatively, you can saw it.

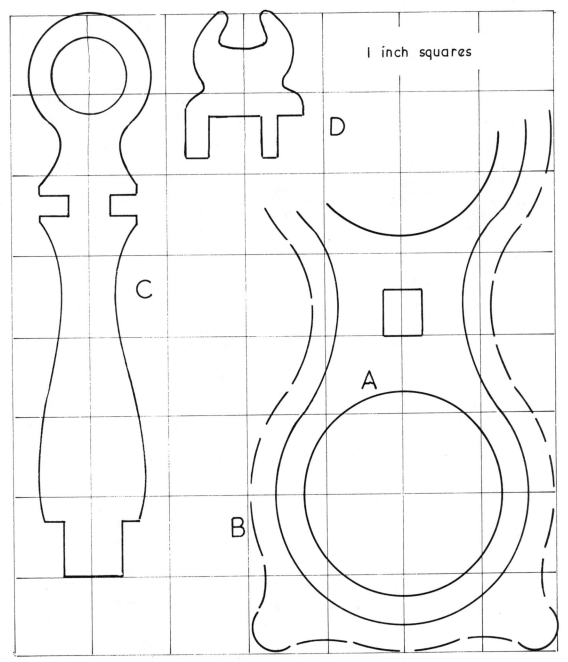

I inch squares

D

C

A

B

Fig. 8-26. Sizes of parts for the pot and spoon stand.

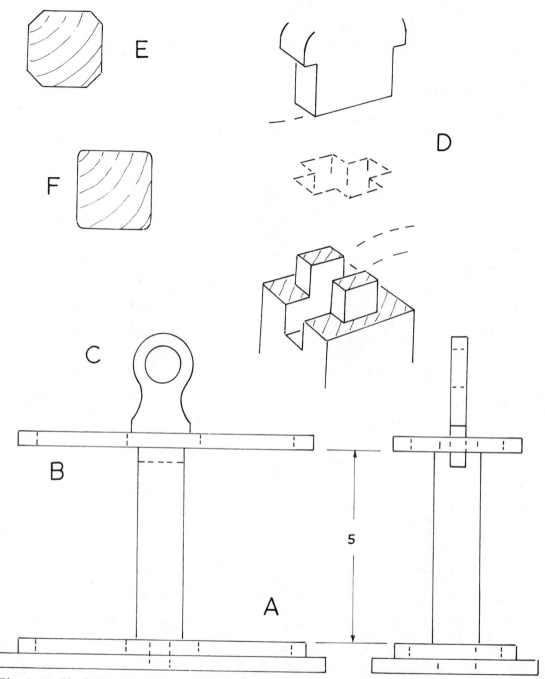

Fig. 8-27. The bottle stand has a central pillar.

Cut the outline completely. Match the tenon to the base mortise. The notches near the top must match the thickness of the wood used for the spoon holders.

In order for the spoon holders to join the handle with adequate strength, they have to be cut to fit into each other (FIG. 8-25B). This allows them to go around the center of the handle with plenty of glue area. Both pieces are the same (FIG. 8-26D). To be certain of an accurate fit, cut the joint parts of one and turn it over on the markings of the other to see that the projections will mate and the space left at the center will go around the handle.

Compare the spoons you intend to use with the drawn racks. Adjust if necessary, but so long as you can pass the narrow neck of the handle through the opening, the bowl of the spoon does not need to be a very close fit in the slot.

Thoroughly round the prominent edges, or you might choose to leave them with just the sharpness sanded off. In any case, round the finger hole and its surrounding area sufficiently to be comfortable.

Glue in two stages. Glue the base parts together. Check that the borders are parallel, and leave under a weight for the glue to set. Join the spoon racks to the handle. See that joints are close and the parts are square. When the glue on these parts has set, join the handle to the base, and check squareness.

The bottle holder (FIG. 8-24B) has a square pillar, but other parts are sheet wood. Many sizes are comparable with the pot and spoon holder, but allow for the differences described below.

Make the two parts of the base (FIG. 8-27A) in the same way as for the other holder, but leave cutting the mortise until you have the pillar ready to compare. The mortise will go crosswise.

The upper parts that holds the bottles (FIG. 8-27B) has holes which match those below, but to give it strength, it has wider rims (FIG. 8-28A). Leave cutting the mortise until other parts are ready to compare.

Make the handle (FIG. 8-27C) in a similar way to the first one, but its base is slightly wider and there is a tenon (FIG. 8-28B).

Two views of the pillar are shown (FIG. 8-28C and D).

At the bottom there is a plain tenon (FIG. 8-28E). Cut a mortise through both parts of the base crosswise to match it.

At the top of the pillar, there is a tenon similar to that at the bottom. Then the tenon of the handle goes across it and a short way into the fullsize part of the pillar (FIG. 8-27D).

Cut the tenon on the pillar (FIG. 8-28F) and mark the mortise crosswise for it (FIG. 8-28G). Mark the mortise for the handle crossing it; then cut through the tenon and go deep enough into the pillar to take the length of the handle tenon (FIG. 8-28H).

After you are satisfied that all joints will fit, either bevel or round the corners of the pillar (FIG. 8-27E and F).

Glue the base parts. Glue the top joint and check squareness. When the glue on these parts has set, join the pillar to the base. See that it is square and the upper part is parallel with the base.

Finish both items with polish or varnish, or use paint.

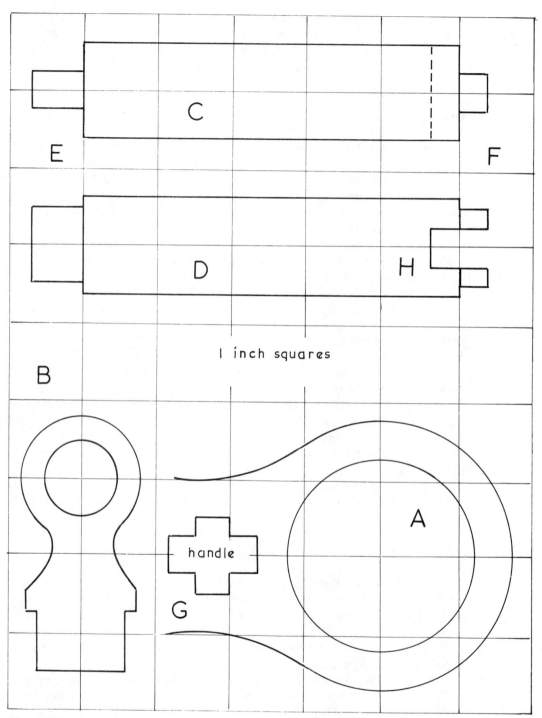

Fig. 8-28. *Sizes of parts of the bottle stand.*

Materials List for Table Servers

1 base	⅜ ×	4 × 11
1 base	⅜ ×	4 × 10
1 handle	½ ×	2 × 8
2 spoon holders	¼ ×	2 × 2
Bottle Holder		
1 base	⅜ ×	4 × 11
1 base	⅜ ×	4 × 10
1 top	⅜ ×	4 × 10
1 handle	½ ×	2 × 4
1 pillar	1¼ ×	1¼ × 8

CUTLERY CARRIER

This portable cutlery rack (FIG. 8-29) has slots for six knives, forks and spoons, with tray space below for several other items. Your cutlery can be stored and then carried to and from your dining table.

All parts are ½-inch wood, which will look best if it is a choice hardwood given a clear finish. This is not a project to make from plywood. Although it would be possible to cut joints, glue and fine nails will be strong enough. The nail heads should be set below the surface and the heads covered with stopping.

As drawn (FIG. 8-30), the cutlery carrier is 9-inches wide, 12-inches high and 14-inches long. It might be compressed a little, and you may find you wish to alter sizes when you compare the sizes of your cutlery with the slots and spacings shown.

Make the two ends first (FIG. 8-30A). Mark on the positions of other parts. Round the edges of the hand holes and the areas around them, but the other edges could be left square, except for removing the sharpness.

Mark out the top (FIG. 8-30B, 31B and 32A). Compare the sizes of slots with your knives, forks and spoons. Spoons and forks can alternate in the outside slots, if yours need more width than is allowed for all one type to go along each side.

Cut the slots. The knife slots might be started by drilling to the full width at each end. Round the outer edges of the top.

The two supports (FIG. 8-31C) are parallel pieces the same length as the top.

The bottom is shown with a shaped edge all round (FIG. 8-31D). The same shaping will be used on the sides. For the sake of uniformity, it is advisable to make a cardboard or hardboard template of one-fourth of the bottom (FIG. 8-32B); use this for marking out all shaped parts. When marking out the bottom, check it against the other parts to see that there will be an even border all round. So that anything inadvertently dropped through a knife slot does not become trapped, cut a slot in the center of the bottom (FIG. 8-31E) to within 2 inches of the end. Anything inside can then be shaken out.

Make the two sides (FIG. 8-30C and 31F), with their lengths the same as the top, and edges the same as the bottom (FIG. 8-32C).

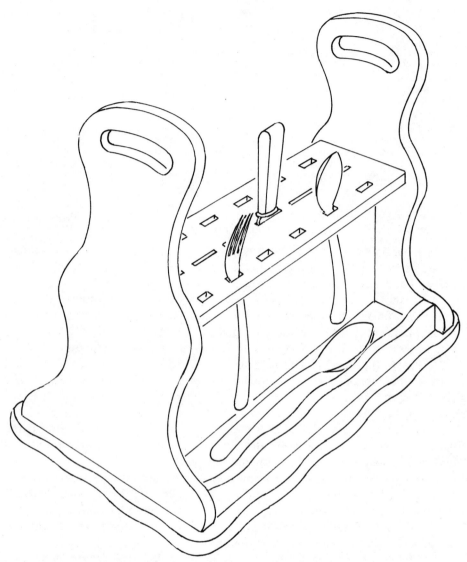

Fig. 8-29. A cutlery stand may be carried by the end handles.

Sand all parts before assembly. First, glue and pin the top to the supports. Fit this assembly between the ends. Check to see there is no twist. Add the bottom and the sides. Punch all pins below the surface, and cover the heads with wood filler before finishing with stain and polish.

Glue cloth under the bottom to protect a polished surface and prevent slipping.

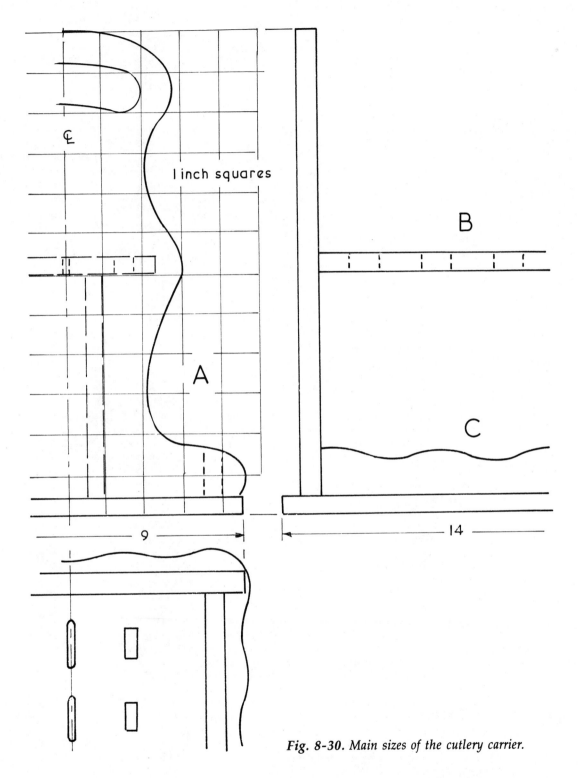

1 inch squares

C_L

A

B

C

9

14

Fig. 8-30. Main sizes of the cutlery carrier.

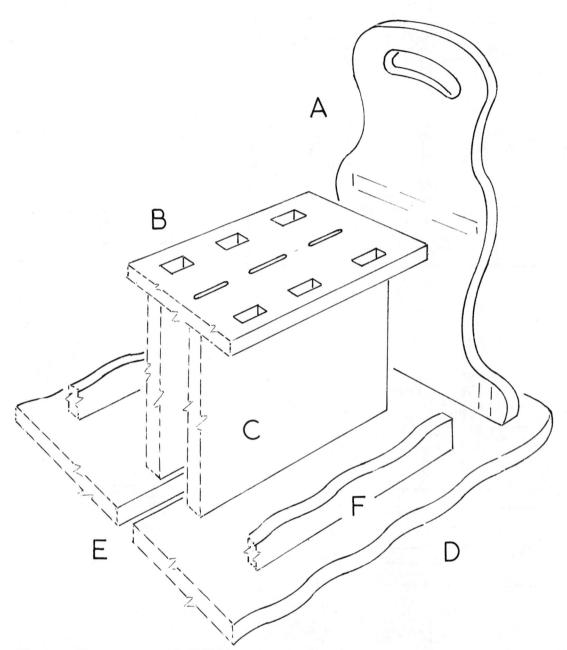

Fig. 8-31. *How the parts of the cutlery stand fit together.*

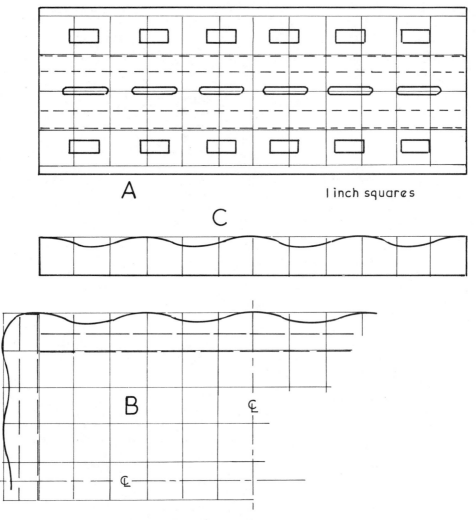

A

1 inch squares

C

B

Fig. 8-32. Sizes of parts of the cutlery carrier.

Materials List for Cutlery Carrier

2 ends	$\frac{1}{2} \times 9 \times 12$
1 top	$\frac{1}{2} \times 4\frac{1}{2} \times 14$
2 supports	$\frac{1}{2} \times 5\frac{1}{2} \times 14$
2 sides	$\frac{1}{2} \times 1 \times 14$
1 bottom	$\frac{1}{2} \times 9 \times 15$

Index

Other Bestsellers of Related Interest

COUNTRY CLASSICS: 25 Early American Projects—Gloria Saberin

If you like to work with wood, you can easily make authentic reproductions of Early American antiques by following the plans in this guide. Each project, selected for its unique charm and simplicity, includes a photo of the finished piece, historical information about the item, materials list, instructions, working plans, and construction tips. A special section of full-color photographs is also included. 184 pages, 198 illustrations, 4 full-color pages. Book No. 3587, $12.95 paperback, $19.95 hardcover

DESIGNING AND BUILDING SPACE-SAVING FURNITURE With 28 Projects—2nd Edition—Percy W. Blandford

In this handy guide from the TAB Furniture Woodshop Series, step-by-step directions, exploded diagrams and two-color illustrations are included with detailed advice on planning and preparing, measuring, woodworking techniques, fasteners, upholstery, and tool usage. You'll find a wealth of easy-to-accomplish projects for increasing storage space in every room in your home. 192 pages, 200 illustrations, 2-color throughout. Book No. 3074, $12.95 paperback, $21.95 hardcover

REFINISHING OLD FURNITURE—George Wagoner

This is the place to look for answers on how to choose the proper finish, make simple repairs, select the best refinishing methods, and care for and touch up your projects. The easy-to-use format includes illustrations, a summary of materials and applications, safety guidelines, addresses for material suppliers, a glossary of refinishing terms, and a list of other helpful books. 192 pages, 96 illustrations. Book No. 3496, $12.95 paperback, $19.95 hardcover

79 FURNITURE PROJECTS FOR EVERY ROOM—Percy W. Blandford

Just imagine your entire home filled with beautiful, handcrafted furniture—elegant chairs, tables, and sofas, a hand-finished corner cupboard, luxurious beds and chests, and more! With the hands-on instructions and step-by-step project plans included here, you'll be able to build beautiful furniture for any room . . . or every room in your home . . . at a fraction of the store-bought cost! 380 pages, 292 illustrations. Book No. 2704, $16.95 paperback, $24.95 hardcover

DESIGNING AND BUILDING COLONIAL AND EARLY AMERICAN FURNITURE, With 47 Projects—2nd Edition—Percy W. Blandford

An internationally recognized expert in the field provides first-rate illustrations and simple instructions on the art of reproducing fine furniture. Every project in this volume is an exquisite reproduction of centuries-old originals: drop-leaf tables, peasant chairs, swivel-top tables, ladder-back chairs, tilt-top box tables, hexagonal candle stands, dry sinks, love seats, Welsh dressers, and more! 192 pages, 188 illustrations. Book No. 3014, $12.95 paperback only

101 OUTSTANDING WOODEN TOY AND CHILDREN'S FURNITURE PROJECTS—Wayne L. Kadar

Turn inexpensive materials into fun and functional toys. Challenge and charm the youngsters in your life with building blocks, pull toys, shape puzzles, stilts, trains, trucks, boats, planes, dolls and more. This step-by-step guide is abundantly illustrated and provides complete materials lists. 304 pages, 329 illustrations. Book No. 3058, $15.95 paperback, $24.95 hardcover

77 ONE-WEEKEND WOODWORKING PROJECTS—Percy W. Blandford

Let this guide put the fun back into your hobby! Overflowing with step-by-step instructions, easy-to-follow illustrations, dimensional drawings, and material lists, this indispensable guide includes plans for 77 projects: tables, racks and shelves, take-down book rack, low bookcase, corner shelves, magazine rack, portable magazine bin, shoe rack, vase stand, beds and cabinets, yard and garden projects, toys, games and puzzles, tools, and more. 304 pages, 226 illustrations. Book No. 2774, $18.95 paperback only

WOODWORKING: Techniques, Tips, & Projects from a Master Craftsman—B. William Bigelow

Here's where the woodworker who's acquired basic skills can learn specialized techniques for using the table saw, the band saw, the wood lathe, the router, and the drill press. Bigelow has chosen 25 projects that illustrate each technique. Each project comes with detailed plans, step-by-step photographs, illustrations of finished pieces, and a listing of tool and material suppliers. 238 pages, 237 illustrations. Book No. 3255, $16.95 paperback, $26.95 hardcover

THE PORTABLE ROUTER BOOK
—R.J. De Christoforo

If you've always thought of your portable router as a pretty unexciting tool, capable of little more than producing decorative edges on certain types of woodworking projects . . . then this book is just what you need to start taking advantage of all the creative possibilities that the router can really offer! Plus, you'll find how-to's for making your own router stands, jigs, fixtures and guides for use in creating such special effects as fluting, reeding, tapering, and peripheral cutting. 368 pages, 466 illustrations. Book No. 2869, $14.95 paperback, $24.95 hardcover

GARDEN TOOLS AND GADGETS YOU CAN MAKE—Percy W. Blandford

This book boasts project plans for just about any garden convenience or accessory you can think of! All of them will make gardening more enjoyable, productive, and easier—you'll be amazed at the money you can save by making your own garden tools. Step-by-step instructions and detailed illustrations accompany each project. Included are small hand tools, boxes, bins, climbing supports, carts, buildings, and more. 260 pages, illustrated. Book No. 3194, $11.95 paperback, $18.95 hardcover

2997